Literature & Thought

THE HARLEM RENAISSANCE

D1318491

Perfection Learning®

EDITORIAL DIRECTOR	Julie A. Schumacher, Carol Francis
SENIOR EDITOR	Rebecca Christian
EDITORS	Lucy Anello
	Ken Sidey
PERMISSIONS	Adam Conley
REVIEWERS	Ruth Ann Gaines
	Mary Gershon
RESEARCH ASSISTANT	Ashley Kuehl

DESIGN AND PHOTO RESEARCH   William Seabright and Associates, Glencoe, Illinois

COVER ART

INTERPRETATION OF HARLEM JAZZ (DETAIL) 1925 Winold Reiss

ACKNOWLEDGMENTS

"All God's Chillun Got Eyes" by E. Franklin Frazier from *The Crisis*. Copyright © April 1924. The Publisher wishes to thank The Crisis Publishing Co., Inc., the publisher of the magazine of the National Association for the Advancement of Colored People, for the use of this work.

"Any Human to Another" by Countee Cullen. Copyrights administered by Thompson and Thompson, New York, NY.

"A Black Man Talks of Reaping" by Arna Bontemps. Reprinted by permission of Harold Ober Associates Incorporated. Copyright © 1963 by Arna Bontemps.

"Black Men, You Shall Be Great Again" by Marcus Garvey from *Philosophy and Opinions of Marcus Garvey* © 1923. Reprinted by permission of The Majority Press, Inc.

"Dream Variation" from *The Collected Poems of Langston Hughes* by Langston Hughes, copyright © 1994 by the estate of Langston Hughes. Used by permission of Alfred A. Knopf, a division of Random House, Inc.

CONTINUED ON PAGE 159

13   14   15   PP   18   17   16   15   14   13

78974
Paperback ISBN: 978-0-7891-5455-2
RLB ISBN: 978-0-7569-0625-2

Printed in the United States of America

WHAT WAS THE
HARLEM RENAISSANCE?

The question above is the *essential question* that you will consider as you read this book. The literature, activities, and organization of the book will lead you to think critically about this question and to develop a deeper understanding of the Harlem Renaissance.

To help you shape your answer to the broad essential question, you will read and respond to four sections, or clusters. Each cluster addresses a specific question and thinking skill.

CLUSTER ONE What was life like during the Harlem Renaissance?
DESCRIBE

CLUSTER TWO What did Harlem Renaissance writers say about being Black? **ANALYZE**

CLUSTER THREE What contributions were made to American art and culture? **GENERALIZE**

CLUSTER FOUR Thinking on your own **SYNTHESIZE**

Notice that the final cluster asks you to think independently about your answer to the essential question—*What was the Harlem Renaissance?*

DREAM VARIATION

To fling my arms wide
In some place of the sun,
To whirl and to dance
Till the white day is done.
Then rest at cool evening
Beneath a tall tree
While night comes on gently,
        Dark like me—
That is my dream!

To fling my arms wide
In the face of the sun,
Dance! whirl! whirl!
Till the quick day is done.
Rest at pale evening. . . .
A tall, slim tree. . . .
Night coming tenderly
        Black like me.

Langston Hughes

TO MIDNIGHT NAN AT LEROY'S
1926
Aaron Douglas

TABLE OF CONTENTS

CLUSTER TWO   WHAT DID HARLEM RENAISSANCE WRITERS SAY ABOUT BEING BLACK?

Thinking Skill   ANALYZING

CLUSTER THREE   WHAT CONTRIBUTIONS WERE MADE TO AMERICAN ART AND CULTURE?

Thinking Skill GENERALIZING

FROM
STILL LIFE IN HARLEM

Eddy L. Harris

came up from the subway and into the bright light of day. I felt a little of what Langston Hughes must have felt when he first arrived in Harlem in 1922. It was a bright September afternoon that greeted me, a bright September afternoon that greeted him. And as he was happy and thrilled to be here, so was I, though probably not as much, for in 1922 Harlem was still young and new and its magic had yet to be tarnished. Langston Hughes was so delirious on coming here, he later wrote, that he was never able to capture on paper the excitement even of riding the subway uptown.

"I went up the steps," he said, *"and out into the bright September sunlight. Harlem! I stood there, dropped my bags, took a deep breath and felt happy again."*

I was happy to be here too. I turned the corner and was excited enough to leap up the stairs and go out, but instead I went slowly. At the bottom of the steps a man was folded against the wall and was sleeping there. I had to step over him before I could go up.

At the top of the steps an old woman, very thin and very shrunken, barred the exit and was begging for spare change.

**Langston Hughes
(1902–1967)**
Best-known poet of the Harlem Renaissance. His work can be found on pages 4, 55, 78, and 105 of this book.

top **James Van Der Zee**
(1886–1983)

Famous photographer who captured the spirit and people of the Harlem Renaissance on film. See his work on pages 16–17, 20, 21, and 61 of this text.

bottom **William H. Johnson**
(1901–1970)

Artist and world traveler whose paintings express the excitement of the Harlem Renaissance as well as the rural south. Examples of his work can be seen on pages 26 and 105.

When I climbed into the light, I took my own deep breath. The air all around the subway entrance smelled of urine.

Clearly this was not the Harlem of 1922.

Still, it was Harlem. Surely some of the old magic remained. And I was excited to be here, in touch at long last with what I had in many ways abandoned. I had come home again.

As I walked the streets that day, my first day in Harlem, I could feel that history—not just on 125th Street but throughout the district. It was like walking through a living museum where someone pushes a button and you hear recordings of sounds and voices and see images of times gone by.

I felt that I was walking among the ghosts of Harlem's past, that I was coming here as they had come here, as Langston Hughes had come and Duke Ellington had come, as they all had come: the washerwoman and the seamstress; the heiress and the showgirl; the hard-laboring man and the vagrant; the high and mighty, the lowly and disregarded; the leaders and the followers; artists and intellectuals—coming home, coming to find peace, coming to gain in Harlem a sense of self and a new way of defining oneself, blackness, black culture, black awareness, that was independent of the white world's limiting influence and strictures and prying eyes. Here they and we and I could live completely within ourselves, in a world all black, all our own and of our own making. Or at least, like the dancing man, we could pretend to.

I felt the weight of Harlem's hope and the rhythms of its excitement. They were all around me, in my ears and in my eyes and upon my shoulders. They stirred in my soul like some half-forgotten memory now suddenly awakened. I felt amazingly free, as if I were really and truly free for the very first time in my life.

At the same time I felt strangely burdened, about as unfree and bound as anyone could be. I felt somehow as if I owed somebody something.

By 1925 Harlem was already the center of a certain universe, spinning in an orbit all its own, attracting other worlds to itself with the gravitational pull of an immense black hole. The August issue of the *Saturday Evening Post* that year noted that Harlem was drawing immigrants "from every country in the world that has a colored population. Ambitious and talented colored youth on every continent look forward to reaching Harlem. It is the Mecca for all those who seek Opportunity with a capital *O*."

Aaron Douglas
(1898–1979)
Artist whose work best portrayed the 'New Negro' spirit of the Harlem Renaissance.
Pages 5, 18, 44, and 75 show his work.

James Weldon Johnson came to Harlem from Florida, Marcus Garvey and Claude McKay came from Jamaica. W.E.B. Du Bois came from New England, Langston Hughes came from Kansas.

They came to Harlem from everywhere; people whose names should be on the tip of your tongue, people you never ever heard of. Businessmen came and racketeers came, profiteers and preachers came, the honest and the fakers. Nella Larsen[1] came. Madame C. J. Walker[2] came. Pig Foot Mary[3] came.

Bessie Smith
(1894–1937)
Singer known as "The Empress of the Blues."

1 **Nella Larsen:** biracial writer of the Harlem Renaissance

2 **Madame C. J. Walker:** Sarah Breedlove Walker was the first African American female millionaire in the United States. Her financial help enabled artists of the Harlem Renaissance to meet and discuss ideas.

3 **Pig Foot Mary:** Mary Dean, a food vendor in Harlem who was known for her fried chicken, pigs' feet, and hot corn.

These came as they all came: seeking better. Some sought fame, some sought fortune, and some sought only the future. All of them sought the freedom that could not be had anywhere but here.

They came to Harlem the same as I had come: because Harlem seemed the place to be, the place where you could lose yourself and at the same time find yourself.

Harlem by then had already become more than a place. It was becoming the metaphor. It was becoming the fiery hot liquid center of black creation, the supernova core of a galaxy in the making.

For the outside world Harlem was quickly setting the tone of the time, those energetic Jazz Age years when the war to end all wars[4] was over and the Great Depression had not yet begun. It was a time of enormous excess. Life seemed good and was getting better

4 **the war to end all wars:** World War I

top **Louis Armstrong**
(1901–1971)
Considered by many to be the greatest jazz trumpet player of all time.

above **Billie Holiday**
(1915–1959)
Legendary jazz singer who worked with Count Basie, Artie Shaw, and her mentor, Louis Armstrong.

right **Jacob Lawrence**
(1917–2000)
Highly successful artist who is best known for his many series of colorful panitings depicting black history. Page 85 shows an example of his painting.

all the time, but after such a war you could never be sure. Better to live for the moment. For those who did, Harlem was nightclubs and liquor and music. For those with a deeper vision, Harlem was the creative spirit of an era. Here, in terms of art and music and literature, was Paris and Berlin of the same era rolled into one, but with one tremendous difference. Here at last were the as yet unknown and unheard voices, not of a generation, however lost and suddenly found, but of an entire people stumbling on untested legs and falteringly learning to walk, squeaking and squawking to find a voice and then to find something to say.

And I was walking among their ghosts. I felt indeed as if I owed them something.

This was Harlem in those long-gone days. It was more than the place to be, it was the place you *had* to be if you were black, the place that called you and where your heart was, even if you never set foot there.

left **Claude McKay** (1890–1948) Jamaican-born Harlem Renaissance poet who often expressed his political ideas through poetry. His work is found on page 44.

below **Zora Neale Hurston** (1891–1960) Author who wrote novels, stories, folklore, and an autobiography. Her most popular work is the novel *Their Eyes Were Watching God*. See works by and about her on pages 63-67 and 119-139.

left **Paul Robeson,** (1898–1976) Renowned actor and singer who became a controversial spokesman against racism.

right **Duke Ellington** (1899–1974) World-famous composer and musician who wrote and recorded hundreds of compositions. Read about him on pages 101–104.

It was a movement at the center of which was the search for a place of equality in American society, equality based on pride and what W.E.B. Du Bois called uplift. Harlem was the seat of the black search for an artistic and intellectual self, the search for identity that emerged during what we now label the Harlem Renaissance, the emergence of black culture to find its soul.

above **Countee Cullen**
(1903–1946)
Poet whose work expressed his views of black life and social issues. Examples of his verse are on pages 45 and 57.

right **Rose McClendon,** (1884–1936)
Playwright and founder of the Negro People's Theatre in Harlem.

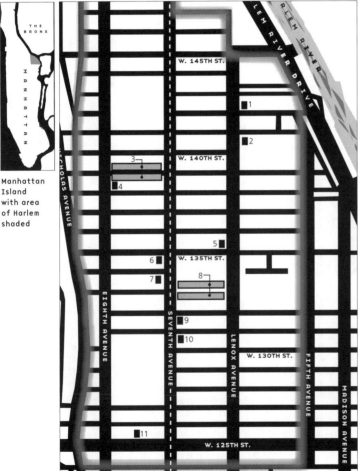

THE BRONX

Manhattan Island with area of Harlem shaded

key to map

1 Cotton Club
2 Savoy Ballroom
3 Stivers Row
4 Pace Phonograph Corp.
5 Schomburg Center
6 Smalls' Paradise
7 St. Philips Episcopal Church
8 Jungle Alley
9 Lafayette Theatre
10 Connie's Inn
11 Apollo Theatre
12 James Van Der Zee studio

Map of Harlem
(1925–1930)
Concentrated area of creative activity in Manhattan during the Harlem Renaissance

CLUSTER ONE

WHAT WAS LIFE LIKE DURING THE HARLEM RENAISSANCE?

Thinking Skill   DESCRIBING

One Hundred Twenty-fifth Street, c. 1930

SEVENTH AVENUE:
THE GREAT BLACK WAY

Jervis Anderson

hen the great bandleader Cab Calloway,[1] who grew up in Rochester and Baltimore, first saw Harlem, in 1929, he was, he said, "awestruck by the whole scene." Never had he beheld "so many Negroes in one place," or a street as glamorous as Seventh Avenue. "It was beautiful," he added. "Just beautiful ... night clubs all over, night clubs whose names were legendary to me." The young Duke Ellington[2]—a native of Washington, D.C.—is said to have remarked on first seeing Harlem, in the early twenties, "Why, it is just like the Arabian Nights."[3]

Seventh Avenue was the most handsome of the boulevards running through Harlem. It was bisected into an uptown and a downtown drive by a narrow strip of park, planted with trees and flowers. Despite the renown and importance of 125th street—the district's main commercial artery—it was Seventh Avenue that deserved to be called the main street of Harlem. It reflected almost every form of life uptown—with its stores, churches, beauty parlors, doctors' offices, theatres, night clubs, nice-looking apartment buildings, and private brownstones.[4] The novelist Wallace Thurman[5]

1 **Cab Calloway:** American composer, bandleader, and singer who gained fame at Harlem's Cotton Club in the 1920s and '30s

2 **Duke Ellington:** famous American composer, bandleader, and pianst who helped found big-band jazz and the swing era, 1899-1974

3 **Arabian Nights:** Arabic tales of wonder

4 **brownstones:** dwellings faced with reddish brown sandstone

5 **Wallace Thurman:** African American editor, critic, novelist, and playwright who lived from 1902-1934

referred to it as Harlem's "most representative" avenue, "a grand thoroughfare into which every element of the Harlem population ventures either for reasons of pleasure or of business." From 125th street to 145th street, he added, Seventh Avenue was "majestic yet warm," and reflected "both the sordid chaos and the rhythmic splendor of Harlem."

In the twenties, Seventh Avenue was the headquarters of Harry Pace's Black Swan phonograph company, which produced some of the earliest recordings of jazz and the blues. On the avenue, there were the Renaissance ballroom and such fine theatres as the Roosevelt, the Alhambra, and the Lafayette. Among the churches there, Salem Methodist was perhaps the largest, and among the cabarets, the most famous were Connie's Inn and Smalls' Paradise. During the thirties,

PARADE ON SEVENTH AVENUE IN HARLEM
James Van Der Zee, photographer

James Van Der Zee,[6] Harlem's best-known photographer, had his studio on the avenue. Of Van Der Zee, a sympathetic and indefatigable recorder of Harlem life, Cecil Beaton wrote in 1938: "In Harlem he is called upon to capture the tragedy as well as the happiness in life, turning his camera on death and marriage with the same detachment." Several of the left-wing ideologues who harangued crowds at the corner of Lenox Avenue and 135th Street edited their little magazines from offices on Seventh. The Blyden Bookstore and the National Bookstore, virtual academies of black consciousness, were on the avenue. Owned by Dr. Willis Huggins and Lewis Michaux, respectively, their stocks leaned heavily to volumes on African and Afro-American history. "If we couldn't find a book anywhere else," a customer of the National Bookstore later said, "we always knew that Michaux had a copy on hand; but perhaps more important than the availability of books was the kind of books he had—books on Africa now out of print; books on the history of *us*." At the corner of Seventh and 125th Street—across the way from Michaux's bookstore—was Harlem's best hotel, the Theresa. It was not until around 1940, however, that the Theresa began admitting blacks, at which point, according to *Ebony*, it became "the social headquarters for Negro America, just as the Waldorf is the home for the white elite." The magazine added: "To its famous registration desk flock the most famous Negroes in America. It is the temporary home of practically every outstanding Negro who comes to New York. . . . Joe Louis stays there, along with every big-time Negro fighter. So does Rochester and the Hollywood

The Crisis COVER
1926
Aaron Douglas

Cab Calloway with his band

6 **James Van Der Zee:** African American photographer whose work chronicled the Harlem Renaissance. His photos can be seen on pages 16-17, 20, 21, and 61 of this text.

contingent, all the top bandleaders who haven't the good fortune to have their own apartments in town, Negro educators, colored writers, and the Liberian and Haitian diplomatic representatives. Big men in the business world jostle top labor leaders in the flowered, mirrored lobby."

To many in Harlem, Seventh Avenue, a boulevard of high style, was "the Great Black Way." One requirement of a grand funeral procession in Harlem was that it

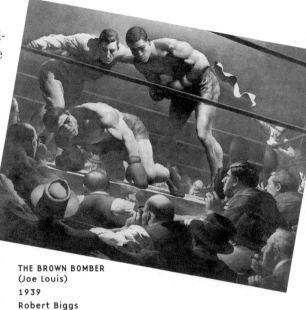

THE BROWN BOMBER
(Joe Louis)
1939
Robert Biggs

make its way up or down Seventh Avenue at some point. Father Divine's religious marches and Marcus Garvey's black nationalist parades—resplendent with colorful banners and uniforms—achieved a special swagger only when, from other streets and thoroughfares, they swung into Seventh Avenue. When the great black fraternal organizations (the Elks, the Odd Fellows, the Monarchs, the Masons, or the Pythians) came to Harlem for an annual convention, a high point of their gathering was an extravaganza of march and music that they staged on Seventh. Perhaps none of these shows was more attractive than the one in 1927, when some thirty thousand lodge brothers and sisters, stepping to the accompaniment of twenty-five marching bands, cakewalked and Charlstoned down the avenue to tunes like "Me and My Shadow" and "Ain't She Sweet."

But Seventh Avenue presented no finer spectacle than its Easter Parades and its Sunday-afternoon promenades, when the high and low of Harlem—in their best clothes or wearing the latest in fashion—strolled leisurely up and down the avenue. Here is what a writer for *The New Yorker* observed on a Sunday in 1926:

> Now that Fifth Avenue is no longer a promenade, only a fashionable procession of shoppers ... we have been seeking elsewhere for a street which still retains the loafing stroll as a tempo.... Seventh Avenue

*between 127th and 134th Streets . . . is still the real thing in prome-
nades. . . . Here the elite of colored New York stroll almost any evening
in a true Sunday-afternoon-in-the-park manner. Here the young men
in evening clothes and jaunty derbies or in more sporting outfits of
spats,[7] colored shirts, trick canes, loiter on the corners or in front
of the theatres and laugh. . . . dusky young school girls go arm in arm,
sometimes four or five abreast. Here old women waddle along, leading
their favorite hound or poodle; and a group of mammies, exchanging
gossip as though in a small-town back yard, mingle with flashy
young flappers[8]. . . . Prosperous old men with heavy gold watch chains
slung ponderously over wide bellies stroll. . . . Harlem takes its ease
on one of the widest and more lovely avenues in the city.*

▲ ● ▲

PORTRAIT OF COUPLE, MAN WITH
WALKING STICK
1929
James Van Der Zee, photographer

On other Sunday afternoons, male strollers were to be seen in silk toppers, homburgs, cutaways, velvet-collared Chesterfields, boutonnieres, monocles, lorgnettes, gaiters, frock coats, and white gloves. Women carried Yankee sand pocketbooks, and wore high-cuffed peek-a-toe slippers, wide-brimmed hats (decorated with flower bouquets), and veils in chartreuse, lime, pink, blue, black, and white. In 1932, a journal in Harlem reported that many women were wearing "sleek black carouls" with "silver fox and sable trimmings" and "white satin or velvet evening frocks, with draped bodies." Waistlines were "anywhere from the hip top to a high empire line." Dresses were trimmed with fur, "kolinsky fur, the preference." Popular that year was a Paris-designed beret, with "a perky feather" shooting skyward. Shoes were generally suede, in various shades of gray. And almost all the women of fashion showed

7 **jaunty derbies. . . spats:** fashions of the twenties; a stiff felt hat with a
narrow brim. . . a cloth or leather covering over the ankle

8 **flappers:** young woman during the World War I years and the 1920's
whose conduct and dress was considered scandalous

signs of having had an "oatmeal facial." Of course, not all the strollers on Seventh Avenue were *that* smart-looking. And not all belonged to the better classes. It was not so hard to spot the prostitutes. Accustomed to their own style of street walking, they could not quite conceal the habitual rhythms of their gait or suppress the erotic insolence of their derrieres. Prosperous pimps and racketeers—at the wheels of expensive automobiles—cruised up and down the avenue, trolling for the attention of the young, the pretty, and the innocent. Men dressed as exquisitely as Adolphe Menjou[9]—the "dicty's,"[10] as such classy types in Harlem were called—shared the stroll with day laborers, elevator operators, and shoeshine boys, whose humbler duds were probably what the cut-rate economies of Delancey Street permitted. Servants of rich Park and Fifth Avenue families wore the hand-me-downs of their employers, striving, with amusing result, to look the part of what they had on. A number of women were out in ensembles that, as any knowing eye could tell, had been put together on their own sewing machines.

The *Age* was surely correct when it said, of a promenade in 1934, that "the creme de la creme"[11] mingled with the "has beens,"[12] the "would-be's," the "four flushers," the "shallow fops,"[13] and the "humble."

But it was the relaxed and neighborly air of the stroll that mattered the most. *

PORTRAIT OF COUPLE WITH RACCOON COATS
AND STYLISH CAR
1932
James Van Der Zee, photographer

9 **Adolphe Menjou:** French film star

10 **dicty's:** well-dressed men

11 **creme de la creme:** French for "the cream of the cream"; the best of all

12 **"has beens":** formerly famous or popular individuals

13 **"shallow fops":** silly, overdressed men

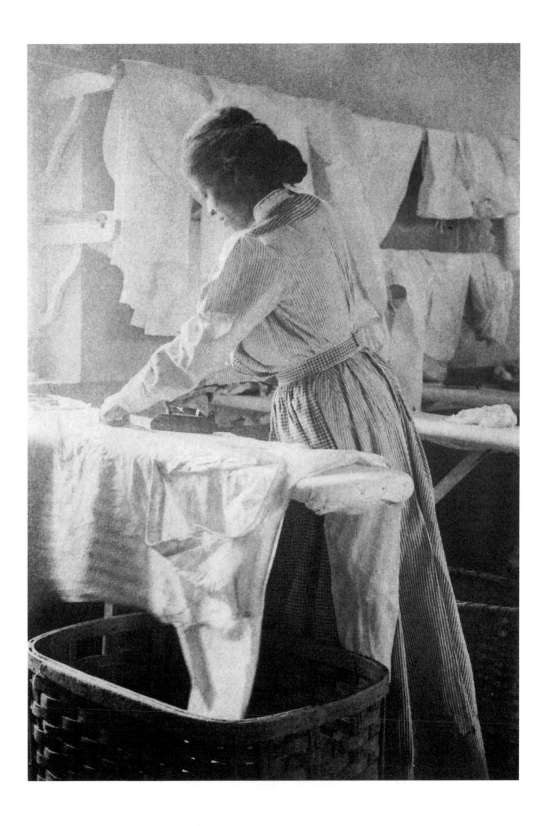

LAUNDRY WORKERS' CHOIR

Vivian Morris

March 9, 1939

It was just about noon, early in March, at the West End Laundry downtown where black women work in the ironing department. The foreman there eyed me suspiciously and then curtly asked me, "What you want?" I showed him a Laundry Workers Union[1] card (which I borrowed from an unemployed laundry worker, in order to ensure my admittance) and told him that I used to work in this laundry and I thought I would drop in and take a friend of mine who worked there out to lunch.

He squinted at the clock and said, "Forty minutes before lunchtime. Too hot in here and how. Better wait outside."

"But," I remonstrated, "the heat doesn't bother me. I used to work in here."

"Say," he ignored my argument, "no fishy back talk and get outside." He watched me until I was out of sight and then he left the room. I promptly darted back into the ironing room where my friend worked.

The clanging of metal as the pistons banged into the sockets, the hiss of steam, women wearily pushing twelve pound irons, women mechanically tending machines—one, button half of the shirt done; two, top finished; three, sleeves pressed and the shirt is ready for the

---

1 **Laundry Workers Union:** an organization established to protect the rights of laundry workers

finishers—that was the scene that greeted me as I stood in the laundry's ironing department.

Shirts, thousands of white shirts that produced such a dazzling glare that the women who work in this department wore dark glasses to protect their eyes. The heat was almost unbearable; there seemed to be gushes of damp heat pushed at you from some invisible force in the mechanism of the machine. The smooth shiny-faced women worked in silence, occasionally dropping a word here and there, slowly wiping away dripping perspiration, then back to the machines, to the heavy irons without any outward show of emotion—no protest. The morning had been long and arduous, this was Wednesday—a heavy day, but thank God half the day was nearly over.

The heavy, strong-armed woman paused the iron, arms unflexed, and glanced at the clock. She smiled. Forty-five minutes until eating time. A soft contralto voice gave vent to a hymn, a cry of protest, as only the persecuted can sing, warm, plaintive, yet with a hidden buoyancy of exultation that might escape a person who has not also felt the pathos and hopes of a downtrodden, exploited people.

She sang, a trifle louder, "Could my tears forever flow, could my zeal no languor know. Thou must save, and thou alone, these fo' sin could not atone; In my hand no price I bring. Simply to his cross I cling."

The women tended their machines to the tempo of the hymn. They all joined in on the chorus, their voices blending beautifully, though untrained and unpolished they voiced the same soulful sentiment, "Rock of Ages, cleft for me. Let me hide myself in thee." Stanza after stanza rang from their lips, voicing oppression centuries old, but the song rang out that the inner struggle for real freedom still lit a fiery spark in the recesses of the souls of these toiling women.

The song ended as it began with soft words and humming. One squat, attractive young woman, who single-handedly handled three of the shirt machines, began a spirited hymn in militant tempo, with a gusto that negated the earlier attitude of fatigue the entire crew of the ironing room joined in either humming or singing. They were entering the final hour before lunch but to judge from the speed that the song had spurred them to, you would believe they were just beginning. The perspiration dripped copiously but it was forgotten. The chorus of the. hymn zoomed forth.

"Dare to be a Daniel.[2] Dare to stand alone. Dare to have a purpose firm and make it known—and make it known."

The woman who finishes the laces with the twelve-pound iron wielded it with feathery swiftness and sang her stanza as the others hummed and put in a word here and there.

"Many a mighty gal is lost darin' not to stand."

The words of the next line were overcome by the rise in the humming, but the last line was clear and resonant.

"By joinin' Daniel's band." The chorus was filled with many pleasing ad-libs and then another took up a stanza. Finally the song died away.

Then the squat machine handler said to the finisher who guided the big iron, "Come on, baby, sing 'at song you made up by yourself. The Heavy Iron Blues." Without further coaxing the girl addressed as "baby" cleared her throat and began singing. "I lift my iron, Lawd, heavy as ton of nails. I lift my i'on, Lawd, heavy as a ton of nails, but it pays my rent cause my man's still layin' in jail. Got the blues, blues, got the heavy i'on blues; but my feet's in good shoes, so doggone the heavy i'on blues." Then she started the second stanza which is equally as light but carried some underlying food for thought. "I lif' my i'on, Lawd, all the livelong day. I lif' my i'on, Lawd, all the livelong day, cause dat furniture bill I know I got to pay, Got the blues, blues, got the heavy i'on blues, but, I pay my union dues, so doggone the heavy i'on blues."

There was a sound of whistles from the direction of the river and the girls dropped whatever they were doing and there were many sighs of relief. Lunchtime. ✷

2 **a Daniel:** In the Bible, Daniel chose not to eat of the king's food as the others did.

THE TYPEWRITER

Dorothy West

In this short story, West depicts the slow deterioration of hope in the lives of Southerners who migrated north in search of a better life. Written at the start of the Harlem Renaissance, "The Typewriter" took second place in the first 0pportunity magazine contest and is significant as one of the period's earliest short stories.

It occurred to him, as he eased past the bulging knees of an Irish wash lady and forced an apologetic passage down the aisle of the crowded car, that more than anything in all the world he wanted not to go home. He began to wish passionately that he had never been born, that he had never been married, that he had never been the means of life's coming into the world. He knew quite suddenly that he hated his flat and his family and his friends. And most of all the incessant thing that would "clatter clatter" until every nerve screamed aloud, and the words of the evening paper danced crazily before him, and the insane desire to crush and kill set his fingers twitching.

He shuffled down the street, an abject little man of fifty-odd years, in an ageless overcoat that flapped in the wind. He was cold, and he hated the North, and particularly Boston, and saw suddenly a barefoot pickaninny sitting on a fence in the hot, Southern sun with a piece of steaming corn bread and a piece of fried salt pork in either grimy hand.

He was tired, and he wanted his supper, but he didn't want the beans, and frankfurters, and light bread that Net would undoubtedly have. That Net had had every Monday night since that regrettable

moment fifteen years before when he had told her—innocently—
that such a supper tasted "right nice. Kinda change from what we
always has."

He mounted the four brick steps leading to his door and pulled at the
bell, but there was no answering ring. It was broken again, and in a
mental flash he saw himself with a multitude of tools and a box of
matches shivering in the vestibule after supper. He began to pound
lustily on the door and wondered vaguely if his hand would bleed if he
smashed the glass. He hated the sight of blood. It sickened him.

Some one was running down the stairs. Daisy probably. Millie would
be at that infernal thing, pounding, pounding. . . . He entered. The chill
of the house swept him. His child was wrapped in a coat. She whispered solemnly, "Poppa, Miz Hicks an' Miz Berry's orful mad. They
gointa move if they can't get more heat. The furnace's birnt out all day.
Mama couldn't fix it." He said hurriedly, "I'll go right down. I'll go right
down." He hoped Mrs. Hicks wouldn't pull open her door and glare at
him. She was large and domineering, and her husband was a bully. If her
husband ever struck him it would kill him. He hated life, but he didn't
want to die. He was afraid of God, and in his wildest flights of fancy
couldn't imagine himself an angel. He went softly down the stairs.

He began to shake the furnace fiercely. And he shook into it every
wrong, mumbling softly under his breath. He began to think back over
his uneventful years, and it came to him as rather a shock that he had
never sworn in all his life. He wondered uneasily if he dared say
"damn." It was taken for granted that a man swore when he tended
a stubborn furnace. And his strongest interjection was "Great balls
of fire!"

The cellar began to warm, and he took off his inadequate overcoat
that was streaked with dirt. Well, Net would have to clean that. He'd be
damned—! It frightened him and thrilled him. He wanted suddenly to
rush upstairs and tell Mrs. Hicks if she didn't like the way he was running things, she could get out. But he heaped another shovelful of coal
on the fire and sighed. He would never be able to get away from himself and the routine of years.

He thought of that eager Negro lad of seventeen who had come
North to seek his fortune. He had walked jauntily down Boylston Street,
and even his own kind had laughed at the incongruity of him. But he

had thrown up his head and promised himself: "You'll have an office here some day. With plate-glass windows and a real mahogany desk." But, though he didn't know it then, he was not the progressive type. And he became successively, in the years, bell boy, porter, waiter, cook, and finally janitor in a down town office building.

He had married Net when he was thirty-three and a waiter. He had married her partly because—though he might not have admitted it— there was no one to eat the expensive delicacies the generous cook gave him every night to bring home. And partly because he dared hope there might be a son to fulfill his dreams. But Millie had come, and after her twin girls who had died within two weeks, then Daisy, and it was tacitly understood that Net was done with child-bearing.

Life, though flowing monotonously, had flowed peacefully enough until that sucker of sanity became a sitting-room fixture. Intuitively at the very first he had felt its undesirability. He had suggested hesitating-ly that they couldn't afford it. Three dollars: food and fuel. Times were hard, and the twenty dollars apiece the respective husbands of Miz Hicks and Miz Berry irregularly paid was only five dollars more than the thirty-five a month he paid his own Hebraic landlord. And the Lord knew his salary was little enough. At which point Net spoke her piece, her voice rising shrill. "God knows I never complain 'bout nothin'. Ain't no other woman got less than me. I bin wearin' this same dress here five years an' I'll wear it another five. But I don't want nothin'. I ain't never wanted nothin'. An' when I does as', it's only for my children. You're a poor sort of father if you can't give that child jes' three dollars a month to rent that typewriter. Ain't 'nother girl in school ain't got one. An' mos' of 'ems bought an' paid for. You know yourself how Millie is. She wouldn't as' me for it till she had to. An' I ain't going to disappoint her. She's goin' to get that typewriter Saturday, mark my words."

On a Monday then it had been installed. And in the months that fol-lowed, night after night he listened to the murderous "tack, tack, tack" that was like a vampire slowly drinking his blood. If only he could escape. Bar a door against the sound of it. But tied hand and foot by the economic fact that "Lord knows we can't afford to have fires burnin' an' lights lit all over the flat. You'all gotta set in one room. An' when y'get tired settin' y'c'n go to bed. Gas bill was somep'n scandalous last month."

He heaped a final shovelful of coal on the fire and watched the first blue flames. Then, his overcoat under his arm, he mounted the cellar stairs. Mrs. Hicks was standing in her kitchen door, arms akimbo. "It's warmin'," she volunteered.

"Yeh," he was conscious of his grime-streaked face and hands, "it's warmin'. I'm sorry 'bout all day."

She folded her arms across her ample bosom. "Tending a furnace ain't a woman's work. I don't blame your wife none 'tall."

Unsuspecting he was grateful. "Yeh, it's pretty hard for a woman. I always look after it 'fore I goes to work, but some days it jes' ac's up."

"Y'oughta have a janitor, that's what y'ought," she flung at him. "The same cullud man that tends them apartments would be willin'. Mr. Taylor has him. It takes a man to run a furnace, and when the man's away all day—"

"I know," he interrupted, embarrassed and hurt, "I know. Tha's right, Miz Hicks tha's right. But I ain't in a position to make no improvements. Times is hard."

She surveyed him critically. "Your wife called down 'bout three times while you was in the cellar. I reckon she wants you for supper."

"Thanks," he mumbled and escaped up the back stairs.

He hung up his overcoat in the closet, telling himself, a little lamely, that it wouldn't take him more'n a minute to clean it up himself after supper. After all Net was tired and prob'bly worried what with Miz Hicks and all. And he hated men who made slaves of their women folk. Good old Net.

He tidied up in the bathroom, washing his face and hands carefully and cleanly so as to leave no—or very little—stain on the roller towel. It was hard enough for Net, God knew.

He entered the kitchen. The last spirals of steam were rising from his supper. One thing about Net she served a full plate. He smiled appreciatively at her unresponsive back, bent over the kitchen sink. There was no one could bake beans just like Net's. And no one who could find a market with frankfurters quite so fat.

He sank down at his place. "Evenin', hon."

He saw her back stiffen. "If your supper's cold, 'tain't my fault. I called and called."

He said hastily, "It's fine, Net, fine. Piping."

She was the usual tired housewife. "Y'oughta et your supper 'fore you fooled with that furnace. I ain't bothered 'bout them niggers. I got all my dishes washed 'cept yours. An' I hate to mess up my kitchen after I once get it straightened up."

He was humble. "I'll give that old furnace an extra lookin' after in the mornin'. It'll las' all day to-morrow, hon."

"An' on top of that," she continued, unheeding him and giving a final wrench to her dish towel, "that confounded bell don't ring. An'—"

"I'll fix it after supper," he interposed hastily.

She hung up her dish towel and came to stand before him looming large and yellow. "An' that old Miz Berry, she claim she was expectin' comp'ny. An' she knows they must 'a' come an' gone while she was in her kitchen an' couldn't be at her winder to watch for 'em. Old liar," she brushed back a lock of naturally straight hair. "She wasn't expectin' nobody."

"Well, you know how some folks are—"

"Fools! Half the world," was her vehement answer. "I'm goin' in the front room an' set down a spell. I bin on my feet all day. Leave them dishes on the table. God knows I'm tired, but I'll come back an' wash 'em." But they both knew, of course, that he, very clumsily, would.

At precisely quarter past nine when he, strained at last to the breaking point, uttering an inhuman, strangled cry, flung down his paper, clutched at his throat and sprang to his feet, Millie's surprised young voice, shocking him to normalcy, heralded the first of that series of great moments that every humble little middle-class man eventually experiences.

"What's the matter, poppa? You sick? I wanted you to help me."

He drew out his handkerchief and wiped his hot hands. "I declare I must 'a' fallen asleep an' had a nightmare. No, I ain't sick. What you want, hon?"

"Dictate me a letter, poppa. I c'n do sixty words a minute.—You know, like a business letter. You know, like those men in your building dictate to their stenographers.[1] Don't you hear 'em sometimes?"

"Oh, sure, I know, hon. Poppa'll help you. Sure. I hear that Mr. Browning—Sure."

---

1 **stenographers:** those who use shorthand to take dictation

Net rose. "Guess I'll put this child to bed. Come on now, Daisy, without no fuss.—Then I'll run up to pa's. He ain't bin well all week."

When the door closed behind them, he crossed to his daughter, conjured the image of Mr. Browning in the process of dictating, so arranged himself, and coughed importantly.

"Well, Millie—"

"Oh, poppa, is that what you'd call your stenographer?" she teased. "And anyway pretend I'm really one—and you're really my boss, and this letter's real important."

A light crept into his dull eyes. Vigor through his thin blood. In a brief moment the weight of years fell from him like a cloak. Tired, bent, little old man that he was, he smiled, straightened, tapped impressively against his teeth with a toil-stained finger, and became that enviable emblem of American life: a business man.

"You be Miz Hicks, huh, honey? Course we can't both use the same name. I'll be J. Lucius Jones. J. Lucius. All them real big doin' men use their middle names. Jus' kinda looks big doin', doncha think, hon? Looks like money, huh? J. Lucius." He uttered a sound that was like the proud cluck of a strutting hen. "J. Lucius." It rolled like oil from his tongue.

His daughter twisted impatiently. "Now, poppa—I mean Mr. Jones, sir—please begin. I am ready for dictation, sir."

He was in that office on Boylston Street, looking with visioning eyes through its plate-glass windows, tapping with impatient fingers on its real mahogany desk.

"Ah—Beaker Brothers, Park Square Building, Boston, Mass. Ah—Gentlemen: In reply to yours at the seventh instant I would state—"

Every night thereafter in the weeks that followed, with Daisy packed off to bed, and Net "gone up to pa's" or nodding inobtrusively in her corner there was the chameleon change of a Court Street janitor to J. Lucius Jones, dealer in stocks and bonds. He would stand, posturing importantly, flicking imaginary dust from his coat lapel, or, his hands locked behind his back, he would stride up and down, earnestly and seriously debating the advisability of buying copper with the market in such a fluctuating state. Once a week, too, he stopped in at Jerry's, and after a preliminary purchase of cheap cigars, bought the latest trade papers, mumbling an embarrassed explanation: "I got a little money. Think I'll invest it in reliable stock."

The letters Millie typed and subsequently discarded, he rummaged for later, and under cover of writing to his brother in the South, laboriously with a great many fancy flourishes, signed each neatly typed sheet with the exalted J. Lucius Jones.

Later, when he mustered the courage he suggested tentatively to Millie that it might be fun—just fun, of course!—to answer his letters. One night—he laughed a good deal louder and longer than necessary— he'd be J. Lucius Jones, and the next night—here he swallowed hard and looked a little frightened—Rockefeller or Vanderbilt or Morgan— just for fun, y'understand! To which Millie gave consent. It mattered little to her one way or the other. It was practice, and that was what she needed. Very soon now she'd be in the hundred class. Then maybe she could get a job!

He was growing very careful of his English. Occasionally—and must be admitted, ashamedly—he made surreptitious ventures into the dictionary. He had to, of course. J. Lucius Jones would never say "Y'got to" when he meant "It is expedient." And, old brain though he was, he learned quickly and easily, juggling words with amazing facility.

Eventually he bought stamps and envelopes—long, important looking envelopes—and stammered apologetically to Millie, "Honey, poppa thought it'd help you if you learned to type envelopes, too. Reckon you'll have to do that, too, when y'get a job. Poor old man," he swallowed painfully, "came round selling these envelopes. You know how 'tis. So I had to buy 'em." Which was satisfactory to Millie. If she saw through her father, she gave no sign. After all, it was practice, and Mr. Hennessey had said that—though not in just those words.

He had got in the habit of carrying those self-addressed envelopes in his inner pocket where they bulged impressively. And occasionally he would take them out—on the car usually—and smile upon them. This one might be from J. P. Morgan. This one from Henry Ford. And a million-dollar deal involved in each. That narrow, little spinster, who, upon his sitting down, had drawn herself away from his contact, was shunning J. Lucius Jones!

Once, led by some sudden, strange impulse, as an outgoing car rumbled up out of the subway, he got out a letter, darted a quick, shamed glance about him, dropped it in an adjacent box, and swung aboard the car, feeling, dazedly, as if he had committed a crime. And the next night he sat in the sitting-room quite on edge until Net said suddenly, "Look here, a real important letter come to-day for you, pa. Here 'tis. What you s'pose it says," and he reached out a hand that trembled. He made brief explanation. "Advertisement, hon. Thassal."

They came quite frequently after that, and despite the fact that he knew them by heart, he read them slowly and carefully, rustling the sheet, and making inaudible, intelligent comments. He was, in these moments, pathetically earnest.

Monday, as he went about his janitor's duties, he composed in his mind the final letter from J. P. Morgan that would consummate a big business deal. For days now letters had passed between them. J. P. had been at first quite frankly uninterested. He had written tersely and briefly. He wrote glowingly of the advantages of a pact between them. Daringly he argued in terms of billions. And at last J. P. had written his next letter would be decisive. Which next letter, this Monday, as he trailed about the office building, was writing itself on his brain.

That night Millie opened the door for him. Her plain face was transformed. "Poppa—poppa, I got a job! Twelve dollars a week to start with! Isn't that swell!"

He was genuinely pleased. "Honey, I'm glad. Right glad," and went up the stairs, unsuspecting.

He ate his supper hastily, went down into the cellar to see about his fire, returned and carefully tidied up, informing his reflection in the bathroom mirror, "Well, J. Lucius, you c'n expect that final letter any day now."

He entered the sitting-room. The phonograph was playing. Daisy was singing lustily. Strange. Net was talking animatedly to—Millie, busy with needle and thread over a neat, little frock. His wild glance darted to the table. The pretty, little centerpiece, the bowl and wax flowers all neatly arranged: the typewriter gone from its accustomed place. It seemed an hour before he could speak. He felt himself trembling. Went hot and cold.

"Millie—your typewriter's—gone!"

She made a deft little in and out movement with her needle. "It's the eighth, you know. When the man came to-day for the money, I sent it back. I won't need it no more—now!—The money's on the mantel-piece, poppa."

"Yeh," he muttered. "All right."

He sank down in his chair, fumbled for the paper, found it.

Net said, "Your poppa wants to read. Stop your noise, Daisy."

She obediently stopped both her noise and the phonograph, took up her book, and became absorbed. Millie went on with her sewing in placid anticipation of the morrow. Net immediately began to nod, gave a curious snort, slept.

Silence. That crowded in on him, engulfed him. That blurred his vision, dulled his brain. Vast, white, impenetrable.... His ears strained for the old, familiar sound. And silence beat upon them.... The words of the evening paper jumbled together. He read: J. P. Morgan goes—

It burst upon him. Blinded him. His hands groped for the bulge beneath his coat. Why this—this was the end! The end of those great moments—the end of everything! Bewildering pain tore through him. He clutched at his heart and felt, almost, the jagged edges drive into his hand. A lethargy swept down upon him. He could not move, nor utter a sound. He could not pray, nor curse.

Against the wall of that silence J. Lucius Jones crashed and died. ✳

ELISE JOHNSON MCDOUGALD
1925
Winold Reiss

STREET SCENE, CHICAGO
1936
Archibald J. Motley, Jr.

RENT PARTIES

Frank Byrd

Due to the rapid influx of tenants to New York from 1910–1924 and to the prejudice of some landlords, African Americans were charged forty to sixty percent more for rent than were white Americans during the Harlem Renaissance. In order to afford the cost of living, rent parties were created in Harlem, a place already known for its celebrations. In the entries that follow, WPA[1] writer Frank Byrd describes the conditions and terms of rent parties in a piece he wrote in 1938.

August 23, 1938

The history of the Harlem house-rent party dates back as far as World War I. To understand what gave such an impetus and community-wide significance to this institution, it is necessary to get a picture of living conditions as they were in Harlem at the time.

During the early 1920s it is estimated that more than 200,000 black people migrated to Harlem: West Indians, Africans, and American blacks from the cotton and cane fields of the Deep South. They were all segregated in a small section of Manhattan about fifty blocks long and seven or eight blocks wide; an area teeming with life and activity. Housing experts have estimated that sometimes as many as 5,000 to 7,000 people have been known to live in a single block.

---

1 **WPA:** Works Progress Administration, created in 1935 by President Franklin D. Roosevelt as a work program for the unemployed

Needless to say, living conditions under such circumstances were anything but wholesome and pleasant. It was a typical slum and tenement area little different from many others in New York except that in Harlem rents were higher; always have been, in fact, since the great wartime migratory influx[2] of colored labor. Despite these exorbitant rents, apartments and furnished rooms, however dingy, were in great demand. Harlem property owners, for the most part Jews, began to live in comparative ease on the fantastic profits yielded by their antiquated dwellings. Before blacks inhabited them, they could be let for virtually a song. Afterward, however, they brought handsome incomes. The tenants, by hook or crook, barely managed to scrape together the rents. In turn they stuck their roomers for enough profit to yield themselves a meager living.

A four- or five-room apartment was (and still is) often crowded to capacity with roomers. In many instances, two entire families occupied space intended for only one family. When bedtime came, there was the feverish activity of moving furniture about, taking down cots, or preparing floor space as sleeping quarters. The same practice of overcrowding was followed by owners or lessees of private houses. Large rooms were converted into two or three small ones by the simple process of strategically placing beaver board partitions. These same cubby holes were rented at the price of full-sized rooms. In many houses, dining and living rooms were transformed into bedrooms soon after, if not before, midnight. Even "shift-sleeping" was not unknown in many places. During the night, a day worker used the room and soon after dawn a night worker moved in. Seldom did the bed have an opportunity to get cold.

In lower Harlem, sometimes referred to as the Latin Quarter and populated mostly by Cubans, Puerto Ricans, and West Indians, accommodations were worse. The Spanish have even less privacy than their American cousins. A three- or four-room apartment often housed ten or twelve people. Parents invariably had the two or three youngest children bedded down in the same room with themselves. The dining room, kitchen, and hallway were utilized as sleeping quarters by relatives or friends.

---

2 **wartime migratory influx:** A large number of Blacks moved north to Harlem during World War I.

Blacks constituted the bulk of the Harlem population, however, and have since the war. At that time, there was a great demand for cheap industrial labor. Strong backed, physically capable blacks from the South were the answer to this demand. They came north in droves, beginning what turned out to be the greatest migration of blacks in the history of the United States. The good news about jobs spread like wildfire throughout the Southlands. There was money, good money, to be made in the north, especially New York. New York—the wondrous, the magical city. The name alone implied glamour and adventure. It was a picture to definitely catch the fancy of restless, overworked sharecroppers[3] and farmhands. And so, it was on to New York, the mecca of the New Negro, the modern Promised Land.

Not only southern, but thousands of West Indian blacks heeded the call. That was the beginning of housing conditions that have been a headache to a succession of political administrations and a thorn in the side of community and civic organizations that have struggled valiantly, but vainly, to improve them.

With the sudden influx of so many blacks, who instinctively headed for Harlem, property that had been a white elephant[4] on the hands of many landlords immediately took an upward swing. The majority of landlords were delighted but those white property owners who made their homes in Harlem were panic-stricken.

At first, there were only rumblings of protest against this unwanted dark invasion but as the tide of color continued to rise, threatening to completely envelop the Caucasian brethren, they quickly abandoned their fight and fled to more remote parts; Brooklyn, Bronx, Queens, and Westchester. As soon as one or two black families moved into a block, the whites began moving out. Then the rents were raised. In spite of this, blacks continued to pour in until there was a solid mass of color in every direction.

Harlemites soon discovered that meeting these doubled, and sometimes tripled, rents was not so easy. They began to think of new ways to meet their ever-increasing deficits. Someone evidently got the idea of having a few friends in as paying party guests a few days before the

3 **sharecroppers:** tenant farmers who maintain others' land and are provided with money for supplies, housing, and food in return

4 **white elephant:** property that requires high maintenance and yields little profit

landlord's scheduled monthly visit. It was a happy timely thought. The guests had a good time and entered wholeheartedly into the spirit of the party. Besides, it cost each individual very little, probably much less than he would have spent in some public amusement place. It became a cheap way to help a friend in need. It was such a good, easy way out of one's difficulties that others decided to make use of it. The Harlem rent party was born.

Like the Charleston and Black Bottom, popular dances of the era, rent parties became an overnight rage. Here at last was a partial solution to the problem of excessive rents and dreadfully subnormal incomes. Family after family and hundreds of apartment tenants opened wide their doors, and went the originators of the idea one better, in fact, by having a party every Saturday night instead of once a month prior to the landlord's call. The accepted admission price became twenty five cents. It was also expected that the guests would partake freely of the fried chicken, pork chops, pigs feet, and potato salad, not to mention homemade "cawn" liquor[5] that was for sale in the kitchen or at a makeshift bar in the hallway.

Saturday night became the night for these galas in Harlem. Some parties even ran well into Sunday morning, calling a halt only after seven or eight o'clock. Parties were eventually held on other nights also. Thursday particularly became a favorite in view of the fact that "sleep in" domestic workers had a day off and were free to kick up their heels without restraint. Not that any other weekday offered Saturday any serious competition. It always retained its popularity because of its all-round convenience as a party day. To begin with, the majority of working-class blacks, maids, porters, elevator operators, and the like were paid on Saturday and, more important than that, were not required to report to work on Sunday. Saturday, therefore, became the logical night to "pitch" and "carry on."

The Saturday night party, like any other universally popular diversion, soon fell into the hands of racketeers. Many small-time pimps and madams who, up to that time, had operated under cover in buffet flats, came out into the open and staged nightly so-called Rent Parties. This, of course, was merely a blind for more illegitimate activities that catered primarily to the desire of traveling salesmen, Pullman porters,

5 **"cawn" liquor:** alcohol made from corn

interstate truck drivers, and other transients for some place to stop and amuse themselves. Additional business could always be promoted from that large army of single or unattached males and females who prowled the streets at night in search of adventure in preference to remaining in their small, dingy rooms in some ill-ventilated flat. There were hundreds of young men and women, fresh from the hinterlands, unknown in New York and eager for the opportunity to meet people. So they would stroll the avenue until they saw some flat with a red, pink, or blue light in the window, the plunk of a tin-panny piano, and sounds of half-tipsy merrymaking fleeting out into the night air; then they would venture in, be greeted volubly by the hostess, introduced around, and eventually steered to the kitchen where refreshments were for sale.

Afterward, there was probably a night filled with continuous drinking, wild, grotesque dancing and crude lovemaking. But it was, at least, a temporary escape from humdrum loneliness and boredom.

The party givers were fully aware of the conditions under which the majority of these boys and girls lived, and decided to commercialize on it as much as possible. They began advertising their get-togethers on little business cards that were naïve attempts at poetic jingles. The following is a typical sample:

> *There'll be brown skin mammas*
> *High yallers too*
> *And if you ain't got nothing to do*
> *Come on up to ROY and SADIE'S*
> *West 126 St. Sat. Night, May 12th.*
> *There'll be plenty of pig feet*
> *An lots of gin*
> *Jus ring the bell*
> *An come on in.*

They were careful, however, to give these cards only to the "right" people. Prohibition was still in effect and the police were more diligent about raiding questionable apartments than they were about known "gin mills" that flourished on almost every corner.

Despite this fact, the number of personal Saturday night responses, in answer to the undercover advertising, was amazing. The party hostess, eager and glowing with freshly straightened hair, would roll back the living room carpets, dim the lights, seat the musicians (usually drummer, piano, and saxophone player), and, with the appearance of the first cash customer, give the signal that would officially get the "rug-cutting" under way. Soon afterward she would disappear into the kitchen in order to give a final, last-minute inspection to the refreshment counter: a table piled high with pig feet, fried chicken, fish, and potato salad.

The musicians, fortified with a drink or two of King Kong (homemade corn whiskey) would begin "beating out the rhythm" on their battered instruments while the dancers kept time with gleeful whoops, fantastic body gyrations and convulsions that appeared to be a cross between the itch and a primitive mating dance.

After some John bought a couple of rounds of drinks, things began to hum in earnest. The musicians instinctively improvised as they went along, finding it difficult, perhaps, to express the full intensity of their emotions through a mere arrangement, no matter how well written.

But the thing that makes the house-rent party (even now) so colorful and fascinating is the unequaled picture created by the dancers themselves. When the band gets hot, the dancers get hotter. They would stir, throw, or bounce themselves about with complete abandon; their wild, grotesque movements silhouetted in the semidarkness like flashes from some ancient tribal ceremony. They apparently worked themselves up into a frenzy but never lost time with the music despite their frantic acrobatics. Theirs is a coordination absolutely unexcelled. It is simple, primitive, inspired. As far as dancing is concerned, there are no conventions. You do what you like, express what you feel, take the lid off[6] if you happen to be in the mood. In short, anything goes.

About one o'clock in the morning; hilarity reaches its peak. "The Boys," most of whom are hard-working, hard-drinking truck drivers, longshoremen, moving men, porters, or laborers, settle down to the serious business of enjoying themselves. They spin, tug, and fling their buxom, amiable partners in all directions. When the music finally stops, they are soaked and steaming with perspiration. "The girls," the majority of whom are cooks, laundresses, maids, or hairdressers, set their hats at a jaunty angle and kick up their heels with glee. Their tan-

---

6 **take the lid off:** slang for "let loose"

talizing grins and the uniformly wicked gleam in their eyes dare the full-blooded young bucks to do their darndest. They may have been utter strangers during the early part of the evening but before the night is over, they are all happily sweating and laughing together in the best of spirits.

Everything they do is free and easy; typical of that group of hard-working blacks [is that] most have few or no inhibitions and the fertility of imagination so necessary to the invention and unrestrained expression of new dance steps and rhythms.

The dancers organize little impromptu contests among themselves and this competition is often responsible for the birth of many new and original dance steps. The house-rent party takes credit for the innovation of the Lindy-Hop that was subsequently improved upon at the Savoy Ballroom. For years, it has been a great favorite with the regular rug-cutting crowd. Nothing has been able to supplant it, not even the Boogie-Woogie that has recently enjoyed a great wave of popularity in uptown New York.

Such unexpected delights as these made the house-rent party, during its infancy, a success with more than one social set. Once in a while a stray ofay (white person) or a small party of pseudo-artistic young blacks, the upper crust, the crème-de-la-crème of Black Manhattan society, would wander into one of these parties and gasp or titter (with cultured restraint, of course) at the primitive, untutored Negroes who apparently had so much fun wriggling their bodies about to the accompaniment of such mad, riotously abandoned music. Seldom, however, did these outsiders seem to catch the real spirit of the party, and as far as the rug-cutters were concerned, they simply did not belong.

With the advent of "Repeal,"[7] the rent party went out, became definitely a thing of the past. Ironically, it was too dangerous to try to sell whiskey after it became legal because the laws regulating its sale were more stringent than those that forbid it to be sold at all.

So, the passing of Prohibition also killed one of the most colorful eras that Harlem, New York, and possibly America, has ever known. ✷

---

7 **"Repeal":** refers to the repeal of Prohibition, a law which prevented the manufacture, sale, or transportation of alcohol in the U.S. from 1919–1933

THE TROPICS IN NEW YORK

Bananas ripe and green, and ginger-root,
Cocoa in pods and alligator pears,
And tangerines and mangoes and grapefruit,
Fit for the highest prize at parish fairs,

Set in the window, bringing memories
Of fruit-trees laden by low-singing rills,[1]
And dewy dawns, and mystical blue skies
In benediction over nun-like hills.

My eyes grew dim, and I could no more gaze;
A wave of longing through my body swept,
And, hungry for the old, familiar ways,
I turned aside and bowed my head and wept.

Claude McKay

1 **rills:** very small streams

HARLEM WINE

This is not water running here,
These thick rebellious streams
That hurtle flesh and bone past fear
Down alleyways of dreams.

This is a wine that must flow on
Not caring how or where,
So it has ways to flow upon
Where song is in the air.

So it can woo an artful flute
With loose, elastic lips,
Its measurement of joy compute
With blithe, ecstatic hips.

BLUES
1929
Archibald J. Motley, Jr.

Responding to Cluster One

What Was Life Like During the Harlem Renaissance?

Thinking Skill DESCRIBING

1. Why do the women sing while they work in "Laundry Workers' Choir"?

2. Why do you think the letters he dictated mean so much to the father in "The Typewriter"?

3. **Define** the term "rent parties." Your definition should include the purpose the parties served.

4. **Sensory images** are descriptive words and phrases that appeal to our senses of touch, taste, smell, sight, and sound. Compare the images in "The Tropics in New York" and "Harlem Wine" by using a chart like the one below.

	The Tropics in New York	Harlem Wine
touch		
taste		
smell		
sight		
sound		

Writing Activity: Creating Word Pictures

Based on what you have read so far, **describe** Harlem and its people as they were during the Harlem Renaissance period. Use sensory images to make your description come alive for the reader.

Strong Descriptive Writing

• avoids clichés.

• uses sensory images to paint a picture for the reader.

CLUSTER TWO

WHAT DID HARLEM RENAISSANCE WRITERS SAY ABOUT BEING BLACK?
Thinking Skill   ANALYZING

PORTRAIT OF W. E. B. DU BOIS

Winold Reiss

ALL GOD'S CHILLUN GOT EYES

E. Franklin Frazier

Being one of God's "chillun," I have eyes. Moreover, being one of his "chillun", I am subject to the ills that befall his children. So, when my eyes which I depend upon constantly indicated strain, I inquired for a specialist in the city. I found that the best specialist was a Scotchman who had come to this country and established himself in the South. His office was on the thirteenth floor of one of those structures to which this city points as a sign of its progress.

Now, in this monument of progress, they have arranged for the preservation of the purity of God's white chillun by having special elevators for God's chillun of my complexion. White people, of course, can ride in the colored elevator, if they are willing to risk momentary contamination, for the sake of dispatch in their business. In short, white people can ride with colored people but colored people are forbidden to ride with white people. Therefore, I was confronted by the problem of having my eyes repaired without damaging my spirit.

Immediately, some white reader will ask the eternal question: "Do you want to be with white people?" My answer is simple. I wanted to get to the thirteenth floor. At that moment, I did not want to be with white people or colored people, tall people or short people, bow-legged people or straight-legged people. I did not even want to go to heaven, while that desire was unfulfilled. There were many things that I did not want, when I attempted to engage in the simple process of getting from one floor to another. I did not want to be reminded my skin was brown. I did not want to hear a lot of foolishness about social equality and racial purity. Above all, I did not want to be marked off as unfit for human association. Enough!

Mount the stairs with me. I am still young and can use my legs and save my self-respect.

The doctor received me cordially, for he soon learned that I was a professor in a college for which he does some work. Immediately, he began to address me by my last name, as if I were his bootblack or office boy, or life-long friend. (I learned afterwards that he had been a very apt student of Southern incivilities). Resentment leaped up within me. Should I protest and let him know that I was simply there on a professional visit and expected the same courtesies accorded other patients? A voice within me reasoned thus: "Be calm, you young fool. Don't you realize that this is the only specialist in the city to take care of you and it is more important that your eyes are treated than that you should teach him a lesson in politeness?" Then the voice whispered: "If you resent, he might put them. . . . No! No! no civilized man could do that. But they have even burned out Negroes' eyes in the South." Realizing the truth of this, I decided to rationalize the situation. This man was simply an ill-bred coward with a veneer of civilization who was afraid to be a gentleman. I was his superior in manners and humanity.

He led me into a room rather dimly lighted by a court and told me to tell the girl who would come in that I was waiting to have drops put into my eyes. Soon, a thin ghostly girl, clothed in black, glided into the room. Evidently a descendant of the noble Anglo-Saxons of the clay hills of Georgia, she had a pallid face, sunken eyes and lips painted a gaudy red. When she filled the eye dropper from one of the three bottles on the shelf, and approached me, I almost shrank from her. Was she sure from which bottle she had taken the fluid? Did she care? I was only a "nigger." Perhaps, she did not want to wait on colored people. I had refrained from antagonizing the doctor. Should I not propitiate this white apparition gliding towards me?

A sign of propitiation among human beings is a smile. A voice spoke out: "You fool, don't you dare smile. It would be all right, if an humble ante-bellum *darky* did so; but you are a young Negro college professor. Don't you know that you are out of the place God fitted you for? Already, you have shown your rebellious spirit by walking up thirteen flights, rather than ride with 'your people.' This is dangerously near a desire for social equality. Have you forgotten that in a town where you taught, white people kicked one of your students unmercifully, because he was accused of smiling at a white girl on the street? In a room with a white woman in the South, a Negro's smile would be equal to an attack." She dropped the fluid into my eyes and left the room triumphantly. Suspense. Uncertainty. . . . Yes, I can still see, and it does not hurt. . . . Do not rejoice too soon. . . . In five minutes, she entered again. She dropped the fluid into my eyes a second time and left the room. . . . The suspense lessens. . . . After repeating this several times, she said in a voice not unkind: "I put it in five times. Didn't I?"

With this ordeal passed, I returned to the doctor, who resumed the examination. Again, he showed the same disregard for common courtesy. As I descended the democratic stairs (white and colored peple can walk down the same stairs) I wondered if going up on a Jim Crow[1] elevator were any worse than letting an ill-bred coward insult you. Well, I suppose as long as all God's chillun got eyes that need attention in this land of white supremacy, in the absence of colored specialists, it will be a choice between blindness and insult and discomfiture. ∗

1 **Jim Crow:** originally a character in an 1880's song; refers to laws or practices in support of segregation

RACE PRIDE

W. E. B. Du Bois

Born William Edward Burghardt Du Bois in 1868, this black American civil rights leader and author was also co-founder of the National Association for the Advancement of Colored People, or NAACP. Du Bois was also a Ph.D. recipient from Harvard University and a social researcher. Clashing with contemporary black leaders who accepted segregation, Du Bois called for immediate and complete racial equality. Toward the end of his life, Du Bois joined the Communist party and moved to Ghana.

ur friends are hard—very hard—to please. Only yesterday they were preaching "Race Pride."

"Go to!" they said, "and be proud of your race."

If we hesitated or sought to explain—"Away," they yelled; "Ashamed-of-Yourself and Want-to-be-White!"

Of course, the Amazing Major is still at it, but do you notice that others say less—because they see that bull-headed worship of any "race," as such, may lead and does lead to curious complications?

For instance: Today Negroes, Indians, Chinese, and other groups, are gaining new faith in themselves; they are beginning to "like" themselves; they are discovering that the current theories and stories of "backward" peoples are largely lies and assumptions; that human genius and possibility are not limited by color, race, or blood. What is this new self-consciousness leading to? Inevitably and directly to distrust and hatred of whites; to demands for self-government, separation, driving out of foreigners: "Asia for the Asiatics," "Africa for the Africans," and "Negro officers for Negro troops!"

No sooner do whites see this unawaited development than they point out in dismay the inevitable consequences: "You lose our tutelage," "You spurn our knowledge," "You need our wealth and technique." They point out how fine is the world role of Elder Brother.[1]

Very well. Some of the darker brethren are convinced. They draw near in friendship; they seek to enter schools and churches; they would mingle in industry—when lo! "Get out," yells the White World—"You're not our brothers and never will be"—"Go away, herd by yourselves"—"Eternal Segregation in the Lord!"

Can you wonder, Sirs, that we are a bit puzzled by all this and that we are asking gently, but more insistently, Choose one or the other horn of the dilemma:

1. Leave the black and yellow world alone. Get out of Asia, Africa, and the Isles. Give us our states and towns and sections and let us rule them undisturbed. Absolutely segregate the races and sections of the world

Or—

2. Let the world meet as men with men. Give utter Justice to all. Extend Democracy to all and treat all men according to their individual desert. Let it be possible for whites to rise to the highest positions in China and Uganda[2] and blacks to the highest honors in England and Texas.

Here is the choice. Which will you have, my masters? ✳

---

1 **Elder Brother:** In the Native American tradition, Elder Brother was the first spirit to live on Earth.

2 **Uganda:** a country in Africa composed primarily of African natives

I, TOO

I, too, sing America.

I am the darker brother.

They send me to eat in the kitchen

When company comes,

But I laugh,

And eat well,

And grow strong.

Tomorrow,

I'll be at the table

When company comes.

Nobody'll dare

Say to me,

"Eat in the kitchen,"

Then.

Besides,

They'll see how beautiful I am

And be ashamed—

I, too, am America.

Langston Hughes

ANY HUMAN TO ANOTHER

The ills I sorrow at
Not me alone
Like an arrow,
Pierce to the marrow,
Through the fat
And past the bone.

Your grief and mine
Must intertwine
Like sea and river,
Be fused and mingle,
Diverse yet single,
Forever and forever.

Let no man be so proud
And confident,
To think he is allowed
A little tent
Pitched in a meadow
Of sun and shadow
All his little own.

Joy may be shy, unique,
Friendly to a few,
Sorrow never scorned to speak
To any who
Were false or true.
Your every grief
Like a blade
Shining and unsheathed
Must strike me down.
Of bitter aloes wreathed,
My sorrow must be laid
On your head like a crown.

Countee Cullen

JIM
Selma Burke

BLACK MEN, YOU SHALL BE GREAT AGAIN

Marcus Garvey

Garvey, founder of the Universal Negro Improvement Association,[1]pp
or UNIA, migrated to Harlem from Jamaica in 1916 and traveled
throughout America, becoming disheartened about oppression and
prejudice. In powerful speeches, he urged his brothers and sisters to
be proud of their race. The charismatic Garvey was convinced that
blacks would never be treated fairly in America, and he advocated
the building of an independent nation for black Americans in
Africa. By the mid-1920s, he had about a million followers. He never
did visit Africa, but his message had lasting effects. What follows
is a statement of Garvey's ideas and beliefs.

It comes to the individual, the race, the nation, once in a lifetime to decide upon the course to be pursued as a career. The hour has now struck for the individual Negro as well as the entire race to decide the course that will be pursued in the interest of our own liberty.

We who make up the Universal Negro Improvement Association have decided that we shall go forward, upward and onward toward the great goal of human liberty. We have determined among ourselves that all barriers placed in the way of our progress must be removed, must be cleared away for we desire to see the light of a brighter day.

The Universal Negro Improvement Association for five years has been proclaiming to the world the readiness of the Negro to carve out

---

1 **Universal Negro Improvement Association:** an organization founded
by Garvey in 1914 that sought to improve black pride through
racial education

a pathway for himself in the course of life.... We are organized for the absolute purpose of bettering our condition, industrially, commercially, socially, religiously and politically. We are organized not to hate other men, but to lift ourselves, and to demand respect of all humanity. We have a program that we believe to be righteous; we believe it to be just, and we have made up our minds to lay down ourselves on the altar of sacrifice for the realization of this great hope of ours, based upon the foundation of righteousness. We declare to the world that Africa must be free, that the entire Negro race must be emancipated from industrial bondage, peonage and serfdom; we make no compromise, we make no apology in this our declaration. We do not desire to create offense on the part of the other races, but we are determined that we shall be heard, that we shall be given the rights to which we are entitled....

Men of the Negro race, let me say to you that a greater future is in store for us; we have no cause to lose hope, to become faint-hearted. We must realize that upon ourselves depend our destiny, our future; we must carve out that future, that destiny, and we who make up the Universal Negro Improvement Association have pledged ourselves that nothing in the world shall stand in our way, nothing in the world shall discourage us, but opposition shall make us work harder, shall bring us closer together so that as one man the millions of us will march on toward the goal that we have set for ourselves.

The new Negro shall not be deceived. The new Negro refuses to take advice from anyone who has not felt with him, and suffered with him. We have suffered for three hundred years, therefore we feel that the time has come when only those who have suffered with us can interpret our feelings and our spirit.

It takes the slave to interpret the feelings of the slave; it takes the unfortunate man to interpret the spirit of his unfortunate brother; and so it takes the suffering Negro to interpret the spirit of his comrade.... There is many a leader of our race who tells us that everything is well, and that all things will work out themselves and that a better day is coming. Yes, all of us know that a better day is coming; we all know that one day we will go home to Paradise, but whilst we are hoping by our Christian virtues to have an entry into Paradise we also realize that we are living on earth, and that the things that are practiced in Paradise are not practiced here. You have to treat this world as the world treats you; we are living in a temporal, material age, an age of activity, an age of racial, national selfishness. What else can you expect but to give back to the world what the world gives to you, and we are calling upon the four hundred million Negroes of the world to take a decided stand, a determined stand, that we shall occupy a firm position; that position shall be an emancipated race and a free nation of our own. We are determined that we shall have a free country; we are determined that we shall have a flag; we are determined that we shall have a government second to none in the world. . . .

When we come to consider this history of man, was not the Negro a power, was he not great once? Yes, honest students of history can recall the day when Egypt, Ethiopia and Timbuctoo[2] towered in their civilizations, towered above Europe, towered above Asia. When Europe was inhabited by a race of cannibals, a race of savages, naked men, heathens and pagans, Africa was peopled with a race of cultured black men, who were masters in art, science and literature; men who were cultured and refined; men who, it was said, were like the gods. Even the great poets of old sang in beautiful sonnets of the delight it was afforded the gods to be in companionship with the Ethiopians. Why, then, should we lose hope? Black men, you were once great; you shall be great again. Lose not courage, lose not faith, go forward. The thing to do is to get organized; keep separated and you will be exploited, you will be robbed, you will be killed. Get organized and you will compel the world to respect you. If the world fails to give you consideration, because you are black men, because you are Negroes, four hundred millions of you shall, through organization, shake the pillars of the universe and bring down creation, even as Samson brought down the temple upon his head and upon the heads of the Philistines.[3]

So Negroes, I say, through the Universal Negro Improvement Association, that there is much to live for. I have a vision of the future, and I see before me a picture of a redeemed Africa, with her dotted cities, with her beautiful civilization, with her millions of happy children, going to and fro. Why should I lose hope, why should I give up and take a back place in this age of progress? Remember that you are

---

2 **Egypt, Ethiopia and Timbuctoo:** countries in Africa

3 **Samson brought down...of the Philistines:** In the Bible, Samson seeks revenge on the Philistines by setting fire to their possessions.

men, that God created you Lords of this creation. Lift up yourselves, men, take yourselves out of the mire and hitch your hopes to the stars; yes, rise as high as the very stars themselves. Let no man pull you down, let no man destroy your ambition, because man is but your companion, your equal; man is your brother; he is not your lord; he is not your sovereign master.... ✳

MARCUS GARVEY IN A UNIA PARADE
1924
James Van Der Zee, photographer

HOW IT FEELS TO BE COLORED ME

Zora Neale Hurston

Known for her bold spirit, Zora Neale Hurston was a premier female author of the Harlem Renaissance. Growing up in Eatonville, Florida, Hurston lived in an all-black community; she used this experience as a basis for her novels, short stories, and retold folk tales. Although Hurston and her work were appreciated during her lifetime, she died in near obscurity.

I am colored but I offer nothing in the way of extenuating circumstances except the fact that I am the only Negro in the United States whose grandfather on the mother's side was not an Indian chief.

I remember the very day that I became colored. Up to my thirteenth year I lived in the little Negro town of Eatonville, Florida. It is exclusively a colored town. The only white people I knew passed through the town going to or coming from Orlando. The native whites rode dusty horses, the Northern tourists chugged down the sandy village road in automobiles. The town knew the Southerners and never stopped cane chewing when they passed. But the Northerners were something else again. They were peered at cautiously from behind curtains by the timid. The more venturesome would come out on the porch to watch them go past and got just as much pleasure out of the tourists as the tourists got out of the village.

The front porch might seem a daring place for the rest of the town, but it was a gallery seat for me. My favorite place was atop the gate-

TWO PUBLIC SCHOOL TEACHERS
1925
Winold Reiss

post. Proscenium box for a born first-nighter.[1] Not only did I enjoy the show, but I didn't mind the actors knowing that I liked it. I usually spoke to them in passing. I'd wave at them and when they returned my salute, I would say something like this: "Howdy-do-well-I-thank-you-where-you-goin'?" Usually automobile or the horse paused at this, and after a queer exchange of compliments, I would probably "go a piece of the way" with them, as we say in farthest Florida. If one of my family happened to come to the front in time to see me, of course negotiations would be rudely broken off. But even so, it is clear that I was the first "welcome-to-our-state" Floridian, and I hope the Miami Chamber of Commerce will please take notice.

During this period, white people differed from colored to me only in that they rode through town and never lived there. They liked to hear me "speak pieces"[2] and sing and wanted to see me dance the parse-me-la, and gave me generously of their small silver for doing these things, which seemed strange to me for I wanted to do them so much that I needed bribing to stop. Only they didn't know it. The colored people gave no dimes. They deplored any joyful tendencies in me, but I was their Zora nevertheless. I belonged to them, to the nearby hotels, to the county—everybody's Zora.

But changes came in the family when I was thirteen, and I was sent to school in Jacksonville. I left Eatonville, the town of the oleanders,[3] as Zora. When I disembarked from the river-boat at Jacksonville, she was no more. It seemed that I had suffered a sea change. I was not Zora of Orange County any more, I was now a little colored girl. I found it out in certain ways. In my heart as well as in the mirror, I became a fast brown—warranted not to rub or run.

▲ ● ▲

But I am not tragically colored. There is no great sorrow dammed up in my soul, nor lurking behind my eyes. I do not mind at all. I do not belong to the sobbing school of Negrohood who hold that nature somehow has given them a lowdown dirty deal and whose feelings are all

1 **Proscenium box for a born first-nighter:** The "procenium" is the wall that separates the stage from the auditorium; this seating is closest to the stage. A "first-nighter" is one who attends the first night of a play.

2 **"speak pieces":** give oral recitations

3 **oleanders:** poisonous evergreen shrubs with fragrant white to red flowers

hurt about it. Even in the helter-skelter skirmish that is my life, I have seen that the world is to the strong regardless of a little pigmentation more or less. No, I do not weep at the world—I am too busy sharpening my oyster knife.

Someone is always at my elbow reminding me that I am the grand-daughter of slaves. It fails to register depression with me. Slavery is sixty years in the past. The operation was successful and the patient is doing well, thank you. The terrible struggle that made me an American out of a potential slave said "On the line!" The Reconstruction said "Get set!"; and the generation before said "Go!" I am off to a flying start and I must not halt in the stretch to look behind and weep. Slavery is the price I paid for civilization, and the choice was not with me. It is a bully adventure and all that I have paid through my ancestors for it. No one on earth ever had a greater chance for glory. The world to be won and nothing to be lost. It is thrilling to think—to know that for any act of mine, I shall get twice as much praise or twice as much blame. It is quite exciting to hold the center of the national stage, with the specta-tors not knowing whether to laugh or to weep.

The position of my white neighbor is much more difficult. No brown specter pulls up a chair beside me when I sit down to eat. No dark ghost thrusts its leg against mine in bed. The game of keeping what one has is never so exciting as the game of getting.

I do not always feel colored. Even now I often achieve the uncon-scious Zora of Eatonville before the Hegira. I feel most colored when I am thrown against a sharp white background.

For instance at Barnard. "Beside the waters of the Hudson" I feel my race. Among the thousand white persons, I am a dark rock surged upon, and overswept, but through it all, I remain myself. When covered by the waters, I am; and the ebb but reveals me again.

▲ • ▲

Sometimes it is the other way around. A white person is set down in our midst, but the contrast is just as sharp for me. For instance, when I sit in the drafty basement that is The New World Cabaret[4] with a white person, my color comes. We enter chatting about any little noth-ing that we have in common and are seated by the jazz waiters. In the

---

4 **The New World Cabaret:** a club in New York City

abrupt way that jazz orchestras have, this one plunges into a number. It loses no time in circumlocutions, but gets right down to business. It constricts the thorax and splits the heart with its tempo and narcotic harmonies. This orchestra grows rambunctious, rears on its hind legs and attacks the tonal veil with primitive fury, rending it, clawing it until it breaks through to the jungle beyond. I follow those heathen—follow them exultingly. I dance wildly inside myself; I yell within, I whoop; I shake my assegai above my head, I hurl it true to the mark yeeeeooww! I am in the jungle and living in the jungle way. My face is painted red and yellow and my body is painted blue. My pulse is throbbing like a war drum. I want to slaughter something—give pain, give death to what, I do not know. But the piece ends. The men of the orchestra wipe their lips and rest their fingers. I creep back slowly to the veneer we call civilization with the last tone and find the white friend sitting motionless in his seat, smoking calmly.

"Good music they have here," he remarks, drumming the table with his fingertips.

Music. The great blobs of purple and red emotion have not touched him. He has only heard what I felt. He is far away and I see him but dimly across the ocean and the continent that have fallen between us. He is so pale with his whiteness then and I am so colored.

▲ ● ▲

At certain times I have no race, I am me. When I set my hat at a certain angle and saunter down Seventh Avenue, Harlem City, feeling as snooty as the lions in front of the Forty-Second Street Library, for instance. So far as my feelings are concerned, Peggy Hopkins Joyce[5] on the Boule Mich with her gorgeous raiment, stately carriage, knees knocking together in a most aristocratic manner, has nothing on me. The cosmic Zora emerges. I belong to no race nor time. I am the eternal feminine with its string of beads.

I have no separate feeling about being an American citizen and colored. I am merely a fragment in the Great Soul that surges within the boundaries. My country, right or wrong.

---

5 **Peggy Hopkins Joyce:** Joyce was a dancer in the Ziegfeld Follies.

Sometimes, I feel discriminated against, but it does not make me angry. It merely astonishes me. How can any deny themselves the pleasure of my company? It's beyond me.

But in the main, I feel like a brown bag of miscellany propped against a wall. Against a wall in company with other bags, white, red and yellow. Pour out the contents, and there is discovered a jumble of small things priceless and worthless. A first-water diamond, an empty spool, bits of broken glass, lengths of string, a key to a door long since crumbled away, a rusty knife-blade, old shoes saved for a road that never was and never will be, a nail bent under the weight of things too heavy for any nail, a dried flower or two still a little fragrant. In your hand is the brown bag. On the ground before you is the jumble it held—so much like the jumble in the bags, could they be emptied, that all might be dumped in a single heap and the bags refilled without altering the content of any greatly. A bit of colored glass more or less would not matter. Perhaps that is how the Great Stuffer of Bags filled them in the first place—who knows? ✳

Zora Neale Hurston

THE PINK HAT

Caroline Bond Day

This hat has become to me a symbol. It represents the respective advantages and disadvantages of my life here. It is at once my magic-carpet, my enchanted cloak, my Aladdin's lamp. Yet it is a plain, rough, straw hat, "pour le sport,"[1] as was [a] recently famous green one.

Before its purchase, life was wont to become periodically flat for me. Teaching is an exhausting profession unless there are wells to draw from, and the soil of my world seems hard and dry. One needs adventure and touch with the main current of human life, and contact with many of one's kind to keep from "going stale on the job." I had not had these things and heretofore had passed back and forth from the town a more or less drab figure eliciting no attention.

Then suddenly one day with the self-confidence bred of a becoming hat, careful grooming, and satisfactory clothes I stepped on to a street car, and lo! the world was reversed. A portly gentleman of obvious rank arose and offered me a seat. Shortly afterwards as I alighted a comely young lad jumped to rescue my gloves. Walking on into the store where I always shopped, I was startled to hear the salesgirl sweetly drawl, "Miss or Mrs.?" as I gave the customary initials. I heard myself answering reassuringly "Mrs." Was this myself? I, who was frequently addressed as "Sarah." For you see this is south of the Mason and Dixon

---

1 **"pour le sport"**: French for "for the sport," meaning that the narrator wore this hat for the fun of it

line,[2] and I am a Negro woman of mixed blood unaccustomed to these respectable prefixes.

I had been mistaken for other than a Negro, yet I look like hundreds of other colored women—yellow-skinned and slightly heavy featured, with frizzy brown hair. My maternal grand-parents were Scotch-Irish and English quadroons; paternal grand-parents Cherokee Indian and full blooded Negro; but the ruddy pigment of the Scotch-Irish ancestry is my inheritance, and it is this which shows through my yellow skin, and in the reflection of my pink hat glows pink. Loosely speaking, I should be called a mulatto[3]—anthropologically speaking. I am a dominant of the white type of the F3 generation[4] of secondary crossings. There is a tendency known to the initiated persons of mixed Negro blood in this climate to "breed white" as we say, propagandists to the contrary notwithstanding. In this sense the Proud Race is, as it were, really dominant. The cause? I'll save that for another time.

Coming back to the hat—when I realized what had made me the recipient of those unlooked for, yet common courtesies, I decided to experiment further.

So I wore it to town again one day when visiting an art store looking for prints for my school room. Here, where formerly I had met with indifference and poor service, I encountered a new girl today who was the essence of courtesy. She pulled out drawer after drawer of prints as we talked and compared from Giotto to Sargent.[5] Yes she agreed that Giorgione[6] had a sweet, worldly taste, that he was not sufficiently appreciated, that Titian[7] did over-shadow him. We went back to Velasquez[8] as the master technician and had about decided on "The Forge of Vulcan"[9] as appropriate for my needs, when suddenly she asked, "but where do you teach?" I answered, and she recognized the

---

2 **Mason and Dixon line:** Originally the line between Maryland and Pennsylvania, this boundary became the dividing line between slave states and free states before the Civil War.

3 **mulatto:** a person of mixed Black and white ancestry

4 **F3 generation:** a term from genetics describing the narrator's mixed ancestry

5 **Giotto to Sargent:** artists; Giotto, Italian painter, 1266-1337; John Singer Sargent, American painter, 1856-1925

6 **Giorgione:** Venetian painter, 1478–1510

7 **Titian:** Venetian painter, 1490–1576

8 **Velasquez:** Spanish painter, 1599–1660

9 **"The Forge of Vulcan":** a painting by Velasquez

name of a Negro university. Well—I felt sorry for her. She had blundered. She had been chatting familiarly, almost intimately with a Negro woman. I spared her by leaving quickly, and murmured that I would send for the package.

My mood forced me to walk—and I walked on and on until I stood at the "curb-market." I do love markets, and at this one they sell flowers as well as vegetables. A feeble old man came up beside me. I noticed that he was near-sighted. "Lady," he began, "would you tell me—is them dahlias or pernies up there?" Then, "market smells so good—don't it?"

I recognized a kindred spirit. He sniffed about among the flowers, and was about to say more—a nice old man—I should have liked to stop and talk with him after the leisurely southern fashion, but he was a white old man—and I moved on hastily.

I walked home the long way and in doing so passed the city library. I thought of my far away Boston—no Abbey nor Puvis de Chauvannes[10] here, no marble stairs, no spirit of studiousness of which I might become a part. Then I saw a notice of a lecture by Drinkwater[11] at the women's club—I was starved for something good—and starvation of body or soul sometimes breeds criminals.

So then I deliberately set out to deceive. Now, I decided, I would enjoy all that had previously been impossible. When necessary I would add a bit of rouge and the frizzy hair (thanks to the marcel) could be crimped into smoothness. I supposed also that a well-modulated voice and assurance of manner would be assets.

So thus disguised, for a brief space of time, I enjoyed everything from the attentions of an expert Chiropodist,[12] to grand opera, avoiding only the restaurants—I could not have borne the questioning eyes of the colored waiters.

I would press on my Aladdin's lamp and presto, I could be comforted with a hot drink at the same soda-fountain where ordinarily I should have been hissed at. I could pull my hat down a bit and buy a ticket to see my favorite movie star while the play was still anew.

10 **Abbey nor Puvis de Chauvannes:** American painter and illustrator; French mural painter

11 **Drinkwater:** John Drinkwater, 1882–1937, English poet, playwright, and critic

12 **Chiropodist:** a doctor that specializes in both hands and feet

I could wrap my enchanted cloak about me and have the decent comfort of ladies' rest-rooms. I could have my shoes fitted in the best shops, and be shown the best values in all of the stores—not the common styles "which all the darkies buy, you know." At one of these times a policeman helped me cross the street. A sales-girl in the most human way once said, "I wouldn't get that Sweetie, you and me is the same style and I know." How warming to be like the rest of the world, albeit a slangy and gum-chewing world!

But it was best of all of an afternoon when it was impossible to correct any more papers or to look longer at my own Lares and Penates,[13] to sit upon my magic-carpet and be transported into the midst of a local art exhibit, to enjoy the freshness of George Inness[14] and the vague charm of Brangwyn,[15] and to see white-folk enjoying Tanner[16]— really nice, likable, folk too, when they don't know one. Again it was good to be transported into the midst of a great expectant throng, awaiting the pealing of the Christmas carols at the Municipal Pageant.[17] One could not enjoy this without compunction however, for there was not a dark face to be seen among all of those thousands of people, and my two hundred bright-eyed youngsters should have been there.

Finally—and the last time that I dared upon my carpet, was to answer the call of a Greek play to be given on the lawn of a State University. I drank it all in. Marvelous beauty! Perfection of speech and gesture on a velvet greensward, music, color, life!

Then a crash came. I suppose I was nervous—one does have "horrible imaginings and present fears" down here, subconscious pictures of hooded figures and burning crosses. Anyway in hurrying out to avoid the crowd, I fell and broke an ankle-bone.

Someone took me home. My doctor talked plaster-casts. "No," I said, "I'll try osteopathy,"[18] but there was no chance for magic now. I was

---

13 **Lares and Penates:** In Roman mythology, Lares are guardian spirits of family ancestors and Penates are guardian spirits of the storeroom and hearth.

14 **George Inness:** American landscape painter, 1825–1894

15 **Brangwyn:** Frank Brangwyn, British painter, 20th century

16 **Tanner:** black American painter, 1859–1937, gained international acclaim for depiction of landscapes and biblical themes

17 **Municipal Pageant:** local Christmas pageant

18 **osteopathy:** the medical practice that concentrates on the relationship between muscles, bones, and organs

home in bed with my family—a colored family—and in a colored section of the town. A friend interceded with the doctor whom I had named. "No," he said, "it is against the rules of the osteopathic association to serve Negroes."

I waited a day—perhaps my foot would be better—then they talked bone-surgery. I am afraid of doctors. Three operations have been enough for me. Then a friend said, "try Christian Science."[19] Perhaps I had been taking matters too much in my own hands, I thought. Yes, that would be the thing. Would she find a practitioner for me?

Dear, loyal daughter of New England—as loyal to the Freedman's children as she had been to them. She tried to spare me. "They will give you absent treatments and when you are better we will go down." I regret now having said, "Where, to the back door?" What was the need of wounding my friend?

Besides, I have recovered some how—I am only a wee bit lame now. And *mirabili dictu!*[20] My spirit has knit together as well as my bones. My hat has grown useless. I am so glad to be well again, and back at my desk. My brown boys and girls have become reservoirs of interest. One is attending Radcliff[21] this year. My neighborly friend needs me now to while away the hours for her. We've gone back to Chaucer[22] and dug out forgotten romances to be read aloud. The little boy next door has a new family of Belgian hares[23] with which we play wonderful games. And the man and I have ordered seed catalogues for spring.

Health, a job, young minds and souls to touch, a friend, some books, a child, a garden, Spring! Who'd want a hat? *

19 **Christian Science:** a religion founded in 1866 that emphasizes healing through faith

20 *mirabili dictu!:* Latin for "Wonderful to say!"

21 **Radcliff:** a college for women that is affiliated with Harvard University

22 **Chaucer:** English poet best known for "The Canterbury Tales"

23 **Belgian hares:** animals similar to rabbits but with longer ears and hind legs

A BLACK MAN TALKS OF REAPING

I have sown beside all waters in my day.
I planted deep, within my heart the fear
The wind or fowl would take the grain away.
I planted safe against this stark, lean year.

I scattered seed enough to plant the land
In rows from Canada to Mexico,
But for my reaping only what the hand
Can hold at once is all that I can show.

Yet what I sowed and what the orchard yields
My brother's sons are gathering stalk and root,
Small wonder then my children glean in fields
They have not sown, and feed on bitter fruit.

Arna Bontemps

UNTITLED
1926
Aaron Douglas

Responding to Cluster Two

What Did Harlem Renaissance Writers Say About Being Black?

Thinking Skill ANALYZING

1. In a chart similar to the one below, write a sentence or two that **analyzes** how each author feels about being a black American based on their stories.

Author	Selection	Attitude
Frazier	All God's Chillun...	
Hurston	How It Feels...	
Day	The Pink Hat	

2. In your opinion, how have things changed since "Race Pride" was written?

3. **Analyze** the persuasive techniques Marcus Garvey used in "Black Men, You Shall Be Great Again."

4. Based on the selections you have read by authors from the Harlem Renaissance, how do you think black Americans felt about Marcus Garvey's suggestion to migrate to Africa in search of complete acceptance?

5. Zora Neale Hurston uses an extended metaphor at the end of her essay, comparing her life to a brown bag. **Analyze** the metaphor line by line, restating her ideas without the poetic language.

6. In the short story by Caroline Bond Day, in what way is the pink hat an "enchanted cloak"?

Writing Activity: Encounter with the Past

If you had been alive during the Harlem Renaissance, which of these authors would you most like to have met? Write at least one paragraph explaining your choice.

For This Exercise

• consider the message of each author.

• think about whether you agree or disagree with each author.

• include what you might talk about and what questions you might ask during the meeting.

CLUSTER THREE

WHAT CONTRIBUTIONS WERE MADE TO AMERICAN ART AND CULTURE?

Thinking Skill   GENERALIZING

THE ASCENT OF ETHIOPIA
1932
Lois Mailou Jones

THE NEGRO ARTIST
AND THE
RACIAL MOUNTAIN

Langston Hughes

Focusing on black urban life, James Langston Hughes was the author of several novels, plays, children's books, and poetry. His first recognized poem, "The Negro Speaks of Rivers," was published just after his high school graduation. Two of his novels were published before he received his college degree. Although he lived in many cities and traveled abroad as a young man, Hughes eventually settled in Harlem, where he became a central figure in the Harlem Renaissance.

One of the most promising of the young Negro poets said to me once, "I want to be a poet—not a Negro poet," meaning, I believe, "I want to write like a white poet"; meaning subconsciously, "I would like to be a white poet"; meaning behind that, "I would like to be white." And I was sorry the young man said that, for no great poet has ever been afraid of being himself. And I doubted then that, with his desire to run away spiritually from his race, this boy would ever be a great poet. But this is the mountain standing in the way of any true Negro art in America—this urge within the race toward whiteness, the desire to pour racial individuality into the mold of American standardization, and to be as little Negro and as much American as possible.

But let us look at the immediate background of this young poet. His family is of what I suppose one would call the Negro middle class: people who are by no means rich yet never uncomfortable nor hungry—smug, contented, respectable folk, members of the Baptist church. The father goes to work every morning. He is a chief steward at a large white club. The mother sometimes does fancy sewing or supervises parties for the rich families of the town. The children go to a mixed school. In the home they read white papers and magazines. And the mother often says, "Don't be like niggers" when the children are bad. A frequent phrase from the father is, "Look how well a white man does things." And so the word white comes to be unconsciously a symbol of all virtues. It holds for the children beauty, morality, and money. The whisper of "I want to be white" runs silently through their minds. This young poet's home is, I believe, a fairly typical home of the colored middle class. One sees immediately how difficult it would be for an artist born in such a home to interest himself in interpreting the beauty of his own people. He is never taught to see that beauty. He is taught rather not to see it, or if he does, to be ashamed of it when it is not according to Caucasian patterns.

For racial culture the home of a self-styled "high-class" Negro has nothing better to offer. Instead there will perhaps be more aping of things white than in a less cultured or less wealthy home. The father is perhaps a doctor, lawyer, landowner, or politician. The mother may be a social worker, or a teacher, or she may do nothing and have a maid. Father is often dark but he has usually married the lightest woman he could find. The family attend a fashionable church where few really colored faces are to be found. And they themselves draw a color line. In the North they go to white theaters and white movies. And in the South they have at least two cars and house "like white folks." Nordic manners, Nordic faces, Nordic hair, Nordic art (if any), and an Episcopal heaven. A very high mountain indeed for the would-be racial artist to climb in order to discover himself and his people.

But then there are the low-down folks, the so-called common element, and they are the majority—may the Lord be praised! The people who have their hip of gin[1] on Saturday nights and are not too important to themselves or the community, or too well fed, or too learned to watch the lazy world go round. They live on Seventh Street in Washington or State Street in Chicago and they do not particularly care whether they are like white folks or anybody else. Their joy runs, bang! into ecstasy. Their religion soars to a shout. Work maybe a little today,

---

1 **hip of gin:** a bottle of alcohol carried in one's belt

rest a little tomorrow. Play awhile. Sing awhile. O, let's dance! These common people are not afraid of spirituals, as for a long time their more intellectual brethren were, and jazz is their child. They furnish a wealth of colorful, distinctive material for any artist because they still hold their own individuality in the face of American standardizations. And perhaps these common people will give to the world its truly great Negro artist, the one who is not afraid to be himself. Whereas the better-class Negro would tell the artist what to do, the people at least let him alone when he does appear. And they are not ashamed of him—if they know he exists at all. And they accept what beauty is their own without question.

Certainly there is, for the American Negro artist who can escape the restrictions the more advanced among his own group would put upon him, a great field of unused material ready for his art. Without going outside his race, and even among the better classes with their "white" culture and conscious American manners, but still Negro enough to be different, there is sufficient matter to furnish a black artist with a lifetime of creative work. And when he chooses to touch on the relations between Negroes and whites in this country with their innumerable overtones and undertones surely, and especially for literature and the drama, there is an inexhaustible supply of themes at hand. To these the Negro artist can give his racial individuality, his heritage of rhythm and warmth, and his incongruous humor that so often, as in the Blues, becomes ironic laughter mixed with tears. But let us look again at the mountain.

A prominent Negro clubwoman in Philadelphia paid eleven dollars to hear Raquel Meller[2] sing Andalusian popular songs. But she told me a few weeks before she would not think of going to hear "that woman," Clara Smith, a great black artist, sing Negro folksongs. And many an upper-class Negro church, even now, would not dream of employing a spiritual in its services. The drab melodies in white folks' hymnbooks are much to be preferred. "We want to worship the Lord correctly and quietly. We don't believe in 'shouting.' Let's be dull like the Nordics," they say, in effect.

The road for the serious black artist, then, who would produce a racial art is most certainly rocky and the mountain is high. Until recent-

2 **Raquel Meller:** a French singer and actress

ly he received almost no encouragement for his work from either white or colored people. The fine novels of Chesnutt go out of print with neither race noticing their passing. The quaint charm and humor of Dunbar's dialect verse brought to him, in his day, largely the same kind of encouragement one would give a sideshow freak (A colored man writing poetry! How odd!) or a clown (How amusing!).

The present vogue in things Negro, although it may do as much harm as good for the budding colored artist, has at least done this: it has brought him forcibly to the attention of his own people among whom for so long, unless the other race had noticed him beforehand, he was a prophet with little honor. I understand that Charles Gilpin[3] acted for years in Negro theaters without any special acclaim from his own, but when Broadway gave him eight curtain calls, Negroes, too, began to beat a tin pan in his honor. I know a young colored writer, a manual worker by day, who had been writing well for the colored magazines for some years, but it was not until he recently broke into the white publications and his first book was accepted by a prominent New York publisher that the "best" Negroes in his city took the trouble to discover that he lived there. Then almost immediately they decided to give a grand dinner for him. But the society ladies were careful to whisper to his mother that perhaps she'd better not come. They were not sure she would have an evening gown.

The Negro artist works against an undertow of sharp criticism and misunderstanding from his own group and unintentional bribes from the whites. "Oh, be respectable, write about nice people, show how good we are," say the Negroes. "Be stereotyped, don't go too far, don't shatter our illusions about you, don't amuse us too seriously. We will pay you," say the whites. Both would have told Jean Toomer not to write *Cane*.[4] The colored people did not praise it. The white people did not buy it. Most of the colored people who did read *Cane* hate it. They are afraid of it. Although the critics gave it good reviews the public remained indifferent. Yet (excepting the work of Du Bois[5]) *Cane*

---

3 **Charles Gilpin:** African American actor, one of the first to be accepted on the mainstream stage

4 **Jean Toomer . . . *Cane*:** American poet and novelist; Toomer's experimental novel that celebrates the Negro

5 **Du Bois:** W. E. B. Du Bois, African-American sociologist and author, an initiator of the National Association for the Advancement of Colored People (NAACP), and editor of the magazine, *The Crisis*

contains the finest prose written by a Negro in America. And like the singing of Robeson, it is truly racial.

But in spite of the Nordicized Negro intelligentsia and the desires of some white editors we have an honest American Negro literature already with us. Now I await the rise of the Negro theater. Our folk music, having achieved world-wide fame, offers itself to the genius of the great individual American composer who is to come. And within the next decade I expect to see the work of a growing school of colored artists who paint and model the beauty of dark faces and create with new technique the expressions of their own soul-world. And the Negro dancers who will dance like flame and the singers who will continue to carry our songs to all who listen—they will be with us in even greater numbers tomorrow.

Most of my own poems are racial in theme and treatment, derived from the life I know. In many of them I try to grasp and hold some of the meanings and rhythms of jazz. I am as sincere as I know how to be in these poems and yet after every reading I answer questions like these from my own people: Do you think Negroes should always write about Negroes? I wish you wouldn't read some of your poems to white folks. How do you find anything interesting in a place like a cabaret? Why do you write about black people? You aren't black. What makes you do so many jazz poems?

But jazz to me is one of the inherent expressions of Negro life in America; the eternal tom-tom beating in the Negro soul—the tom-tom of revolt against weariness in a white world, a world of subway trains, and work, work, work; the tom-tom of joy and laughter, and pain swallowed in a smile. Yet the Philadelphia clubwoman is ashamed to say that her race created it and she does not like me to write about it. The old subconscious "white is best" runs through her mind. Years of study under white teachers, a lifetime of white books, pictures, and papers, and white manners, morals, and Puritan standards made her dislike the spirituals. And now she turns up her nose at jazz and all its manifestations—almost everything else distinctly racial. She doesn't care for the Winold Reiss[6] portraits of Negroes because they are "too Negro." She does not want a true picture of herself from anybody. She wants the

---

6 **Winold Reiss:** Harlem Renaissance painter (1886-1953).
Examples of his work can be seen on the cover as well as
pages 35, 47, 62, 78, and 107.

artist to flatter her, to make the white world believe that all Negroes are as smug and as near white in soul as she wants to be. But, to my mind, it is the duty of the younger Negro artist, if he accepts any duties at all from outsiders, to change through the force of his art that old whispering "I want to be white," hidden in the aspirations of his people, to "Why should I want to be white? I am a Negro—and beautiful."

So I am ashamed for the black poet who says, "I want to be a poet, not a Negro poet," as though his own racial world were not as interesting as any other world. I am ashamed, too, for the colored artist who runs from the painting of Negro faces to the painting of sunsets after the manner of the academicians because he fears the strange un-whiteness of his own features. An artist must be free to choose what he does, certainly, but he must also never be afraid to do what he might choose.

Let the blare of Negro jazz bands and the bellowing voice of Bessie Smith[7] singing Blues penetrate the closed ears of the colored near-intellecutal until they listen and perhaps understand. Let Paul Robeson singing "Water Boy," and Rudolph Fisher writing about the streets of Harlem, and Jean Toomer holding the heart of Georgia in his hands, and Aaron Douglas drawing strange black fantasies cause the smug Negro middle class to turn from their white, repectable, ordinary books and papers to catch a glimmer of their own beauty. We younger Negro artists who create now intend to express our individual dark-skinned selves without fear or shame. If white people are pleased we are glad. If they are not, it doesn't matter. We know we are beautiful. And ugly too. The tom-tom cries and the tom-tom laughs. If colored people are pleased we are glad. If they are not, their displeasure doesn't matter either. We build our temples for tomorrow, strong as we know how, and we stand on top of the mountain, free within ourselves. ✳

---

7 **Bessie Smith:** African American blues singer, dancer, and actress

ROOFTOPS (NO. 1, THIS IS HARLEM)
1943
Jacob Lawrence

MISS CYNTHIE

Rudolph Fisher

For the first time in her life somebody had called her "madam."

She had been standing, bewildered but unafraid, while innumer-able Red Caps[1] appropriated piece after piece of the baggage arrayed on the platform. Neither her brief seventy years' journey through life nor her long two days' travel northward had dimmed the lively brightness of her eyes, which, for all their bewilderment, had accurately selected her own treasures out of the row of luggage and guarded them vigilantly.

"These yours, madam?"

The biggest Red Cap of all was smiling at her. He looked for all the world like Doc Crinshaw's oldest son back home. Her little brown face relaxed; she smiled back at him.

"They got to be. You all done took all the others."

He laughed aloud. Then— "Carry 'em in for you?"

She contemplated his bulk. "Reckon you can manage it—puny little feller like you?"

Thereupon they were friends. Still grinning broadly, he surrounded himself with her impedimenta, the enormous brown extension-case on one shoulder, the big straw suitcase in the opposite hand, the carpet-bag under one arm. She herself held fast to the umbrella.

"Always like to have sump'm in my hand when I walk. Can't never tell when you'll run across a snake."

"There aren't any snakes in the city."

1 **Red Caps:** porters or baggage carriers

TAPDANCING NEGRO
1914
Ernst Ludwig Kirchner

SHORT STORY   **87**

"There's snakes everywhere, chile."

They began the tedious hike up the interminable platform. She was small and quick. Her carriage was surprisingly erect, her gait astonishingly spry. She said:

"You liked to took my breath back yonder, boy, callin' me 'madam.' Back home everybody call me 'Miss Cynthie.' Even my own chillun. Even their chillun. Black folks, white folks too. 'Miss Cynthie.' Well, when you come up with that 'madam' o' yourn, I say to myself, 'Now, I wonder who that chile's a-grinnin' at? 'Madam' stand for mist'ess o' the house, and I sho' ain' mist'ess o' nothin' in this hyeh New York."

"Well, you see, we call everybody 'madam.' "

"Everybody?—Hm." The bright eyes twinkled. "Seem like that'd worry me some—if I was a man."

He acknowledged his slip and observed, "I see this isn't your first trip to New York."

"First trip any place, son. First time I been over fifty mile from Waxhaw. Only travelin' I've done is in my head. Ain' seen many places, but I's seen a passel o' people. Reckon places is pretty much alike after people been in 'em awhile."

"Yes, ma'am. I guess that's right."

"You ain' no reg'lar bag-toter, is you?"

"Ma'am?"

"You talk too good."

"Well, I only do this in vacation-time. I'm still in school."

"You is. What you aimin' to be?"

"I'm studying medicine."

"You is?" She beamed. "Aimin' to be a doctor, huh? Thank the Lord for that. That's what I always wanted my David to be. My grandchile hyeh in New York. He's to meet me hyeh now."

"I bet you'll have a great time."

"Mussn't bet, chile. That's sinful. I tole him 'fo' he left home, I say, 'Son, you the only one o' the chillun what's got a chance to amount to sump'm. Don' th'ow it away. Be a preacher or a doctor. Work yo' way up and don' stop short. If the Lord don' see fit for you to doctor the soul, then doctor the body. If you don' get to be a reg'lar doctor, be a tooth-doctor. If you jes' can't make that, be a foot-doctor. And if you don' get that fur, be a undertaker. That's the least you must be. That ain' so bad. Keep you acquainted with the house of the Lord. Always mind the house o' the Lord—whatever you do, do like a church steeple: aim high and go straight.' "

"Did he get to be a doctor?"

"Don' b'lieve he did. Too late startin', I reckon. But he's done succeeded at sump'm. Mus' be at least a undertaker, 'cause he started sendin' the home-folks money, and he come home las' year dressed like Judge Pettiford's boy what went off to school in Virginia. Wouldn't tell none of us 'zackly what he was doin', but he said he wouldn't never be happy till I come and see for myself. So hyeh I is." Something softened her voice. "His mammy died befo' he knowed her. But he was always sech a good chile—" The something was apprehension. "Hope he *is* a undertaker."

They were mounting a flight of steep stairs leading to an exit-gate, about which clustered a few people still hoping to catch sight of arriving friends. Among these a tall young brown-skinned man in a light grey suit suddenly waved his panama[2] and yelled, "Hey, Miss Cynthie!"

Miss Cynthie stopped, looked up, and waved back with a delighted umbrella. The Red Cap's eyes lifted too. His lower jaw sagged.

"Is that your grandson?"

"It sho' is," she said and distanced him for the rest of the climb. The grandson, with an abandonment that superbly ignored onlookers, folded the little woman in an exultant, smothering embrace. As soon as she could, she pushed him off with breathless mock impatience.

"Go 'way, you fool, you. Aimin' to squeeze my soul out my body befo' I can get a look at this place?" She shook herself into the semblance of composure. "Well. You don' look hungry, anyhow."

"Ho-ho! Miss Cynthie in New York! Can y'imagine this? Come on. I'm parked on Eighth Avenue."

The Red Cap delivered the outlandish luggage into a robin's egg blue open Packard with scarlet wheels, accepted the grandson's dollar and smile, and stood watching the car roar away up Eighth Avenue.

Another Red Cap came up. "Got a break, hey, boy?"

"Dave Tappen himself—can you beat that?"

"The old lady hasn't seen the station yet—starin' at him."

"That's not the half of it, bozo. That's Dave Tappen's grandmother. And what do you s'pose she hopes?"

2 **panama:** a straw hat

"What?"

"She hopes that Dave has turned out to be a successful undertaker!"

"Undertaker? Undertaker!"

They stared at each other a gaping moment, then doubled up with laughter.

▲ ● ▲

"Look—through there—that's the Chrysler Building. Oh, hell-elujah! I meant to bring you up Broadway—"

"David—"

"Ma'am?"

"This hyeh wagon yourn?"

"Nobody else's. Sweet buggy, ain't it?"

"David—you ain't turned out to be one of them moonshiners, is you?"

"Moonshiners—? Moon—Ho! No indeed, Miss Cynthie. I got a better racket 'n that."

"Better which?"

"Game. Business. Pick-up."

"Tell me, David. What is yo' racket?"

"Can't spill it yet, Miss Cynthie. Rather show you. Tomorrow night you'll know the worst. Can't you make out till tomorrow night?"

"David, you know I always wanted you to be a doctor, even if 'twasn' nothin' but a foot-doctor. The very leas' I wanted you to be was a undertaker."

"Undertaker! Oh, Miss Cynthie!—with my sunny disposition?"

"Then you ain' even a undertaker?"

"Listen, Miss Cynthie. Just forget 'bout what I am for awhile. Just till tomorrow night. I want you to see for yourself. Tellin' you will spoil it. Now stop askin', you hear?—because I'm not answerin'—I'm surprisin' you. And don't expect anybody you meet to tell you. It'll mess up the whole works. Understand? Now give the big city a break. There's the elevated train going up Columbus Avenue. Ain't that hot stuff?"

Miss Cynthie looked. "Humph!" she said. "Tain' half high as that trestle two mile from Waxhaw."

▲ ● ▲

She thoroughly enjoyed the ride up Central Park West. The stagger lights, the extent of the park, the high, close, kingly dwellings, remarkable because their stoves cooled them in summer as well as heated them in winter, all drew nods of mild interest. But what gave her special delight was not these: it was that David's car so effortlessly sped past the headlong drove of vehicles racing northward.

They stopped for a red light; when they started again their machine leaped forward with a triumphant eagerness that drew from her an unsuppressed "Hot you, David! That's it!"

He grinned appreciatively. "Why, you're a regular New Yorker already."

"New Yorker nothin'! I done the same thing fifty years ago—befo' I knowed they was a New York."

"What!"

" 'Deed so. Didn' I use to tell you 'bout my young mare, Betty? Chile, I'd hitch Betty up to yo' grandpa's buggy and pass anything on the road. Betty never knowed what another horse's dust smelt like. No 'ndeedy. Shuh, boy, this ain' nothin' new to me. Why that broke-down Fo'd you' uncle Jake's got ain' nothin'—nothin' but a sorry mess. Done got so slow I jes' won' ride in it—I declare I'd rather walk. But this hyeh thing, now, this is right nice." She settled back in complete, complacent comfort, and they sped on, swift and silent.

Suddenly she sat erect with abrupt discovery.

"David—well—bless my soul!"

"What's the matter, Miss Cynthie?"

Then he saw what had caught her attention. They were traveling up Seventh Avenue now, and something was miraculously different. Not the road; that was as broad as ever, wide, white gleaming in the sun. Not the houses; they were lofty still, lordly, disdainful, supercilious. Not the cars; they continued to race impatiently onward, innumerable, precipitate, tumultuous. Something else, something at once obvious and subtle, insistent, pervasive, compelling.

"David—this mus' be Harlem!"

"Good Lord, Miss Cynthie—!"

"Don' use the name of the Lord in vain, David."

"But I mean—gee!—you're no fun at all. You get everything before a guy can tell you."

"You got plenty to tell me, David. But don' nobody need to tell me this. Look a yonder."

Not just a change of complexion. A completely dissimilar atmosphere. Sidewalks teeming with leisurely strollers, at once strangely dark and bright. Boys in white trousers, berets, and green shirts, with slickened black heads and proud swagger. Bareheaded girls in crisp organdie dresses, purple, canary, gay scarlet. And laughter, abandoned strong Negro laughter, some falling full on the ear, some not heard at all, yet sensed—the warm life-breath of the tireless carnival to which Harlem's heart quickens in summer.

"This is it," admitted David. "Get a good eyeful. Here's One Hundred and Twenty-fifth Street—regular little Broadway. And here's the Alhambra, and up ahead we'll pass the Lafayette."

"What's them?"

"Theatres."

"Theatres? Theatres. Humph! Look, David—is that a colored folks church?" They were passing a fine gray-stone edifice.

"That? Oh. Sure it is. So's this one on this side."

"No! Well, ain' that fine? Splendid big church like that for colored folks."

Taking his cue from this, her first tribute to the city, he said, "You ain't seen nothing yet. Wait a minute."

They swung left through a side-street and turned right on a boulevard. "What do you think o' that?" And he pointed to the quarter-million-dollar St. Mark's.

"That a colored church, too?"

" 'Tain' no white one. And they built it themselves, you know. Nobody's hand-me-down gift."

She heaved a great happy sigh. "Oh, yes, it was a gift, David. It was a gift from on high." Then, "Look a hyeh—which a one you belong to?"

"Me? Why, I don't belong to any—that is, none o' these. Mine's over in another section. Y'see, mine's Baptist. These are all Methodist. See?"

"M-m. Uh-huh. I see."

They circled a square and slipped into a quiet narrow street overlooking a park, stopping before the tallest of the apartment-houses in the single commanding row.

Alighting, Miss Cynthie gave this imposing structure one sidewise, upward glance, and said, "Y'all live like bees in a hive, don't y'?—I boun' the women does all the work, too." A moment later, "So this is a elevator? Feel like I'm glory-bound sho' nuff."

Along a tiled corridor and into David's apartment. Rooms leading into rooms. Luxurious couches, easy-chairs, a brown-walnut grand piano, gay-shaded floor lamps, panelled walls, deep rugs, treacherous glass-wood floors—and a smiling golden-skinned girl in a gingham house-dress, approaching with outstretched hands.

"This is Ruth, Miss Cynthie."

"Miss Cynthie!" said Ruth.

They clasped hands. "Been wantin' to see David's girl ever since he first wrote us 'bout her."

"Come—here's your room this way. Here's the bath. Get out of your things and get comfy. You must be worn out with the trip."

"Worn out? Worn out? Shuh. How you gon' get worn out on a train? Now if 'twas a horse, maybe, or Jake's no-'count Fo'd—but a train—didn' but one thing bother me on that train."

"What?"

"When the man made them beds down, I jes' couldn' manage to undress same as at home. Why, s'posin' sump'm bus' the train open—where'd you be? Naked as a jay-bird in dew-berry time."

David took in her things and left her to get comfortable. He returned, and Ruth, despite his reassuring embrace, whispered:

"Dave, you can't fool old folks—why don't you go ahead and tell her about yourself? Think of the shock she's going to get—at her age."

David shook his head. "She'll get over the shock if she's there looking on. If we just told her, she'd never understand. We've got to railroad her into it. Then she'll be happy."

"She's nice. But she's got the same ideas as all old folks—"

"Yea—but with her you can change 'em. Specially if everything is really all right. I know her. She's for church and all, but she believes in good times too, if they're right. Why, when I was a kid—" he broke off. "Listen!"

Miss Cynthie's voice came quite distinctly to them, singing a jaunty little rhyme:

"Oh I danced with the gal with the hole in her stockin',
And her toe kep' a-kickin' and her heel kep' a-knockin'—

Come up, Jesse, and get a drink o' gin,
'Cause you near to the heaven as you'll ever get ag'in."

"She taught me that when I wasn't knee-high to a cricket," David said.

Miss Cynthie still sang softly and merrily:

"Then I danced with the gal with the dimple in her cheek,
And if she'd 'a' kep' a-smilin', I'd a' danced for a week—"

"God forgive me," prayed Miss Cynthie as she discovered David's purpose the following night. She let him and Ruth lead her, like an early Christian martyr, into the Lafayette Theatre. The blinding glare of the lobby produced a merciful self-anaesthesia, and she entered the sudden dimness of the interior as involutarily as in a dream—

Attendants outdid each other for Mr. Dave Tappen. She heard him tell them, "Fix us up till we go on," and found herself sitting between Ruth and David in the front row of a lower box. A miraculous device of the devil, a motion-picture that talked, was just ending. At her feet the orchestra was assembling. The motion-picture faded out amid a scattered round of applause. Lights blazed and the orchestra burst into an ungodly rumpus.

She looked out over the seated multitude, scanning row upon row of illumined faces, black faces, white faces, yellow, tan, brown; bald heads, bobbed heads, kinky and straight heads; and upon every countenance, expectancy,—scowling expectancy in this case, smiling in that, complacent here, amused there, commentative elsewhere, but everywhere suspense, abeyance, anticipation.

Half a dozen people were ushered down the nearer aisle to reserved seats in the second row. Some of them caught sight of David and Ruth and waved to them. The chairs immediately behind them in the box were being shifted. "Hello, Tap!" Miss Cynthie saw David turn, rise, and shake hands with two men. One of them was large, bald and pink, emanating good cheer; the other short, thin, sallow with thick black hair and a sour mien. Ruth also acknowledged their greeting. "This is my grandmother," David said proudly. "Miss Cynthie, meet my managers, Lou and Lee Goldman." "Pleased to meet you," managed Miss Cynthie. "Great lad, this boy of yours," said Lou Goldman. "Great little partner he's got, too," added Lee. They also settled back expectantly.

"Here we go!"

The curtain rose to reveal a cotton-field at dawn. Pickers in blue denim overalls, bandanas, and wide-brimmed straws, or in gingham aprons and sunbonnets, were singing as they worked. Their voices, from clearest soprano to richest bass, blended in low concordances, first simply humming a series of harmonies, until, gradually, came words, like figures forming in mist. As the sound grew, the mist cleared, the words came round and full, and the sun rose bringing light as if in answer to the song. The chorus swelled, the radiance grew, the two, as if emanating from a single source, fused their crescendos, till at last they achieved a joint transcendence of tonal and visual brightness.

"Swell opener," said Lee Goldman.

"Ripe," agreed Lou.

David and Ruth arose. "Stay here and enjoy the show, Miss Cynthie. You'll see us again in a minute."

"Go to it, kids," said Lou Goldman.

"Yea—burn 'em up," said Lee.

Miss Cynthie hardly noted that she had been left, so absorbed was she in the spectacle. To her, the theatre had always been the antithesis of the church. As the one was the refuge of righteousness, so the other was the stronghold of transgression. But this first scene awakened memories, captured and held her attention by offering a blend of truth and novelty. Having thus baited her interest, the show now proceeded to play it like the trout through swift-flowing waters of wickedness. Resist as it might, her mind was caught and drawn into the impious subsequences.

The very music that had just rounded out so majestically now distorted itself into ragtime. The singers came forward and turned to dancers; boys, a crazy, swaying background, threw up their arms and kicked out their legs in a rhythmic jamboree; girls, an agile, brazen foreground, caught their skirts up to their hips and displayed their copper calves, knees, thighs, in shameless, incredible steps. Miss Cynthie turned dismayed eyes upon the audience, to discover that mob of sinners devouring it all with fond satisfaction. Then the dancers separated and with final abandon flung themselves off the stage in both directions.

Lee Goldman commented through the applause, "They work easy, them babies."

"Yea," said Lou. "Savin' the hot stuff for later."

Two black-faced cotton-pickers appropriated the scene, indulging in dialogue that their hearers found uproarious,

"Ah'm tired."

"Ah'm hongry."

"Dis job jes' wears me out."

"Starves me to death."

"Ah'm so tired—you know what Ah'd like to do?"

"What?"

"Ah'd like to go to sleep and dream I was sleepin'. "

"What good dat do?"

"Den I could wake up and still be 'sleep."

"Well y'know what Ah'd like to do?"

"No. What?"

"Ah'd like to swaller me a hog and a hen."

"What good dat do?"

"Den Ah'd always be full o' ham and eggs."

"Ham? Shuh. Don't you know a hog has to be smoked 'fo' he's a ham?"

"Well, if I swaller him, he'll have a smoke all around him, won' he?"

Presently Miss Cynthie was smiling like everyone else, but her smile soon fled. For the comics departed, and the dancing girls returned, this time in scant travesties on their earlier voluminous costumes—tiny sunbonnets perched jauntily on one side of their glistening bobs, bandanas reduced to scarlet neck-ribbons, waists mere brassieres, skirts mere gingham sashes.

And now Miss Cynthie's whole body stiffened with a new and surpassing shock; her bright eyes first widened with unbelief, then slowly grew dull with misery. In the midst of a sudden great volley of applause her grandson had broken through that bevy of agile wantons and begun to sing.

He too was dressed as a cotton-picker, but a Beau Brummel among cotton-pickers; his hat bore a pleated green band, his bandana was silk, his overalls blue satin, his shoes black patent leather. His eyes flashed, his teeth gleamed, his body swayed, his arms waved, his words came fast and clear. As he sang, his companions danced a concerted tap, uniformly wild, ecstatic. When he stopped singing, he himself began to dance, and without sacrificing crispness of execution, seemed to absorb into himself every measure of the energy which the girls, now merely standing off and swaying, had relinquished.

"Look at that boy go," said Lee Goldman.

"He ain't started yet," said Lou.

But surrounding comment, Dave's virtuosity, the eager enthusiasm of the audience were all alike lost on Miss Cynthie. She sat with stricken eyes watching this boy whom she'd raised from a babe, taught right from wrong, brought up in the church, and endowed with her prayers, this child whom she had dreamed of seeing a preacher, a regular doctor, a tooth-doctor, a foot-doctor, at the very least an undertaker—sat watching him disport himself for the benefit of a sinsick, flesh-hungry mob of lost souls, not one of whom knew or cared to know the loving kindness of God; sat watching a David she'd never foreseen, turned tool of the devil, disciple of lust, unholy prince among sinners.

For a long time she sat there watching with wretched eyes, saw portrayed on the stage David's arrival in Harlem, his escape from "old friends" who tried to dupe him; saw him working as a trap-drummer in a night-club, where he fell in love with Ruth, a dancer; not the gentle Ruth Miss Cynthie knew, but a wild and shameless young savage who danced like seven devils—in only a girdle and breastplates; saw the two of them join in a song-and-dance act that eventually made them Broadway headliners, an act presented *in toto*[3] as the pre-finale of this show. And not any of the melodies, not any of the sketches, not all the comic philosophy of the tired-and-hungry duo, gave her figure a moment's relaxation or brightened the dull defeat in her staring eyes. She sat apart, alone in the box, the symbol, the epitome of supreme failure. Let the rest of the theatre be riotous, clamoring for more and more of Dave Tappen, "Tap," the greatest tapster of all time, idol of uptown and downtown New York. For her, they were lauding simply an exhibition of sin which centered about her David.

"This'll run a year on Broadway," said Lee Goldman.

---

3 *in toto:* on the whole; entirely; totally

"Then we'll take it to Paris."

Encores and curtains with Ruth, and at last David came out on the stage alone. The clamor dwindled. And now he did something quite unfamiliar to even the most consistent of his followers. Softly, delicately, he began to tap a routine designed to fit a particular song. When he had established the rhythm, he began to sing the song:

"Oh I danced with the gal with the hole in her stockin',
And her toe kep' a-kickin' and her heel kep' a-knockin'

Come up, Jesse, and get a drink o' gin,
'Cause you near to the heaven as you'll ever get ag'in—"

As he danced and sang this song, frequently smiling across at Miss Cynthie, a visible change transformed her. She leaned forward incredulously, listened intently, then settled back in limp wonder. Her bewildered eyes turned on the crowd, on those serried[4] rows of shriftless sinners. And she found in their faces now an overwhelmingly curious thing: a grin, a universal grin, a gleeful and sinless grin such as not the nakedest chorus in the performance had produced. In a few seconds, with her own song, David had dwarfed into unimportance, wiped off their faces, swept out of their minds every trace of what had seemed to be sin; had reduced it all to mere trivial detail and revealed these revelers as a crowd of children, enjoying the guileless antics of another child. And Miss Cynthie whispered her discovery aloud:

"Bless my soul! They didn't mean nothin' . . . They jes' didn't see no harm in it—"

"Then I danced with the gal with the dimple in her cheek,
And if she'd 'a' kep' a-smilin' I'd 'a' danced for a week—

Come up, Jesse—"

The crowd laughed, clapped their hands, whistled. Someone threw David a bright yellow flower. "From Broadway!"

He caught the flower. A hush fell. He said:

"I'm really happy tonight, folks. Y'see this flower? Means success, don't it? Well, listen. The one who is really responsible for my success

4 **serried:** crowded or pressed together

is here tonight with me. Now what do you think o' that?"

The hush deepened.

"Y'know folks, I'm sump'm like Adam—I never had no mother. But I've got a grandmother. Down home everybody calls her Miss Cynthie. And everybody loves her. Take that song I just did for you. Miss Cynthie taught me that when I wasn't knee-high to a cricket. But that wasn't all she taught me. Far back as I can remember, she used to always say one thing: 'Son, do like a church steeple—aim high and go straight.' And for doin' it—" he grinned, contemplating the flower—"I get this."

He strode across to the edge of the stage that touched Miss Cynthie's box. He held up the flower.

"So y'see, folks, this isn't mine. It's really Miss Cynthie's." He leaned over to hand it to her. Miss Cynthie's last trace of doubt was swept away. She drew a deep breath of revelation; her bewilderment vanished, her redoubtable composure returned, her eyes lighted up; and no one but David, still holding the flower toward her, heard her sharply whispered reprimand:

"Keep it, you fool you. Where's yo' manners—givin' 'way what somebody give you?"

David grinned:

"Take it, tyro.[5] What you tryin' to do—crab[6] my act?"

Thereupon, Miss Cynthie, smiling at him with bright, meaningful eyes, leaned over without rising from her chair, jerked a tiny twig off the stem of the flower, then sat decisively back, resolutely folding her arms, with only a leaf in her hand.

"This'll do me," she said.

▲ ● ▲

The finale didn't matter. People filed out of the theatre. Miss Cynthie sat awaiting her children, her foot absently patting time to the orchestra's jazz recessional. Perhaps she was thinking, "God moves in a mysterious way," but her lips were unquestionably forming the words:

"—danced with the gal—hole in her stockin'—
—toe kep' a-kickin'—heel kep' a-knockin'—" ✳

---

5 **tyro:** amateur; beginner
6 **crab:** spoil, ruin

FROM
ELLINGTON'S "MOOD IN INDIGO"

Janet Mabie

His name is Edward Kennedy Ellington. Too heavy and somber a name for a dance-band conductor to tote about with him. But that has been taken care of. Somewhere along the road people began to call him "Duke" and the name has stuck. I shouldn't wonder if it is connected somehow with what is quite apparently Ellington's great gift for understanding and his capacity for a very simple kind of friendliness. You would know he had those gifts if you watched him come into the Harlem restaurant [Cotton Club] whence he broadcasts late at night. People take quite appreciable pleasure when he comes in. They smile, and pat their hands together, and say among themselves, "And now we shall hear something."

Duke Ellington's musical career has something very naïve about it. He started out in the most modest fashion you can think of. Born in Washington, he took common school education through high school. Yes, his father played, and his mother played. "Played with music," Duke Ellington says, and you perceive that he has made a very subtle distinction indeed. They played, evidently, so that the playing, lacking the hard brilliance of technically experienced players, stuck in the boy's thought and helped him.

"When I was very young I took piano." An immemorial phrase, to conjure the picture of a child led protestingly to a piano and told there to school himself in an art. "But I couldn't get interested. Not in Czerny[1] and the little things of Bach. Still, I drifted back into it; I played

---

1 **Czerny:** Austrian pianist and composer, 1791–1857

'stomps' when I was 14. Then a pianist in Washington, Oliver Perry, very kindly took an interest in me when he chanced somewhere to hear me. He had a dance band and since he could get more work if he had more men, he broke me in to a sort of apprenticeship.[2] It didn't cost him much and it was an advantage to me too. I was drawing and painting some, and I got a scholarship somehow for more instruction in art; but somewhere, inside of me, something said that was not the thing for me either. So I stayed with Perry.

"Then there was a man named Grant. Henry Grant. He was supervisor of music in the Washington schools. He said he would teach me harmony. I had a kind of harmony inside me, which is part of my race, but I needed the kind of harmony which has no race at all but is universal. So you see, from both those men I received, freely and generously, more than I could ever have paid for. I repaid them as I could; by playing for Mr. Perry, and by learning all I could from Mr. Grant.

"Then I came across a stumbling block. I really couldn't play very well the things white people played. So I decided that, since I must play, I should have to write something I could play myself. I suppose that is the beginning of my compositions. When you are doing things they don't seem milestones to you, but I guess having to write some things I myself could play properly was a milestone for me."

Ellington had a certain conscience about the scholarship in those early fine arts days. "I did all I could, though I knew I couldn't make a career of it. I studied hard at illustration, modeling, and wood carving. Well, it is something to put away in your knowledge, that sort of thing."

The war [World War I] came and in Washington there were parties for charity and war chests.[3] A man named [Louis] Thomas practically controlled the music for the parties and Ellington went to work for him. But, he said ingenuously, "We seemed to have a little trouble about money, so I just took some men, and what music I had managed to get together and, by a lot of us looking over the few sheets of music and picking out the orchestration rather as we went along, we made the music do until we had earned enough money to buy some more music

2 **apprenticeship:** a position held by an inexperienced individual under the direction of an expert

3 **war chests:** money collected to finance a war

and get together some more instruments. And, if you will believe it, we began to make money."

In 1923, there was a man named [Wilbur] Sweatman who wanted Ellington to come to New York, where there was an opportunity for such work. At first he made records for Brunswick; two years ago he went under exclusive contract to Victor.

There is a point of similarity between Duke Ellington and Paul Robeson.[4] Both believe that in the heart of the Africa a man can travel into today there lies a great secret of music. Both want to go there and

Ellington at the piano

4 **Paul Robeson:** African American actor and singer, 1898–1976

find it. I should think it was possible that one day both of them will do it.

Ellington's music is very interesting; sometimes too preponderantly brass; sometimes surprising in its velvety dusk of tone. It is a little hard to get precisely at what he means when he says he wants to "develop legitimate humor" because wailing and moaning and the hollow laughter of brass instruments is debatable humor. From jazz, as a subject, he shies as if he had suddenly touched something red hot. I can't say that I blame him. One way and another you cannot try to dissect jazz, as a phase of music. Too many people have pawed it over and changed it from a simple question for leisurely discussion into something that, at times, I have seen transformed into all the making of a nice brisk little war. "I get very confused," Ellington said, "if people ask me about jazz," and very wisely let it go at that.

Something was said about Ellington's own "Mood in Indigo" ["Mood Indigo"]. I got him to play it for me. I had heard it just once before, on the radio. It had seemed to me, of its kind, a sort of thing just a little too pungently lovely to be quite sure you've actually heard it.

"But it is very simple," he said, when he had finished playing it. "It is just one of those very simple little things that you throw together. Of course, the arrangement makes it. But it really isn't anything; the melody isn't. It's funny, I threw that together, and it has caught on. I've worked desperately over things, and then they haven't come out at all. Isn't it queer, not to have anything for a great deal of work, and something for no work at all?"

Yes, I suppose the "Mood in Indigo" is simple. Very simple indeed if you know how to do it.

"I am just getting a chance to work out some of my own ideas of Negro music. I stick to that. We as a race have a good deal to pay our way with in a white world. The tragedy is that so few records have been kept of the Negro music of the past. It has to be pieced together so slowly. But it pleases me to have a chance to work at it." ✳

JAZZONIA

Oh, silver tree!
Oh, shining rivers of the soul!

In a Harlem cabaret
Six long-headed jazzers play.
A dancing girl whose eyes
    are bold
Lifts high a dress of silken
    gold.

Oh, singing tree!
Oh, shining rivers of the soul!

Were Eve's eyes
In the first garden
Just a bit too bold?
Was Cleopatra gorgeous
In a gown of gold?

Oh, shining tree!
Oh, silver rivers of the soul!

In a whirling cabaret
Six long-headed jazzers play.

Langston Hughes

JITTERBUGS (III)
1941
William H. Johnson

RESPONDING TO CLUSTER THREE

WHAT CONTRIBUTIONS WERE MADE TO AMERICAN ART AND CULTURE?

Thinking Skill GENERALIZING

1. From what you have read and what you know, write a one-sentence **generalization** about the contributions of Harlem Renaissance artists to American art and culture.

2. Based on the Ellington interview, how do you think Duke Ellington might view today's rap and hip–hop musicians?

3. Why did Miss Cynthie disapprove of her grandson's performance? Find three examples that show she changed her mind by the end of the story.

4. You have already read one essay and four poems by Langston Hughes. As a class or in small groups, create a word web like the one below that **generalizes** about Hughes. Put his name in the center of the web. Branches might include topics such as personality, attitudes, and writing.

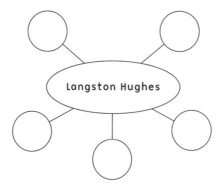

Writing Activity: Musical Poetry

Langston Hughes wrote intimately about his feelings toward jazz in his poem "Jazzonia." Now it's your turn. Write a short poem about your favorite type of music. To write a poem, begin by choosing a topic, feeling, attitude, or belief that you feel strongly about. Think about whether or not you want your poem to rhyme, if it will have a shape, and what tone it will take (angry, happy, sad, sarcastic, etc.).

An Effective Poem

• relates the writer's feelings.

• creates word pictures.

• uses imagery based on taste, touch, sight, sound, and smell.

CLUSTER FOUR

THINKING ON YOUR OWN
Thinking Skill   SYNTHESIZING

DAWN IN HARLEM

1925

Winold Reiss

Spike Lee editing film

SPIKE'S GOTTA DO IT

Spike Lee

*In 1986 Spike Lee released his first feature film; he wrote, directed,
and co-starred in* She's Gotta Have It, *which was shot in Brooklyn
for just $175,000. The black-and-white film was successful,
grossing $8 million in theaters and launching Lee's career.*

FEBRUARY 1, 1985

I have to have at least $75,000 in the bank when we start.... There are
no guarantees in the film industry. People should hope to regain their
investments, that's the first step. Hope you don't lose you shirt.

I will not give up casting or final cut for the investors. That's bottom
line. If they can't live with that, FORGET IT.

This development with AFI has really sobered me up quick. *She's
Gotta Have It* is far from being a lock. I don't have the money so I don't
have a picture. Another thing, the actors do not need to know about the
financial situation. It's hard enough just trying to act.

FEBRUARY 18, 1985

IDEA. The scene where Jamie and Nola meet should be a semi-chase
scene. Jamie is following her, then he loses her. He walks then she ends
up following him. He stops and says, "Are you following me?" Nola:
"You were following me." "Oh, I was. I was struck by your appearance.
I know it sounds corny but if I didn't follow you I know I might not ever
see you again." Nola: "Was it worth it?" Jamie: "Don't know yet. What's
your name?" Nola: "Nola." Jamie: "Nola, I like you. Would you care to

spend some time with me? Maybe a movie or something?" A smile covers his face. Jamie: "You will? Solid."

APRIL 1, 1985

It's becoming apparent that these people I've sent the scripts to won't give me the money. I'm gonna have to raise the money myself with a limited partnership. I have to do it myself, with anybody who will help. It will be a miracle if I can raise the money to shoot in July. One thing, though, I will not become discouraged, I will keep on pushing. I might have to find a job that pays something in the meantime.

APRIL 12, 1985

IDEA. The first time the character of Mars Blackmon is introduced we want to have close-ups of

1. Nike sneakers with fat laces
2. earring
3. gold medallion
4. name belt buckle
5. part in hair
6. Cazals glasses

All of this stuff will be the OFFICIAL B-BOY ATTIRE.

APRIL 25, 1985

In a couple of days the month of May will be here and after that June. Time is moving fast and summer is fast approaching. Either people are gonna get behind me or they won't. It's as simple as that. It's put-up-or-shut-up time. I've just got to get that $53,180 minus my $12,100 which is $41,080, to get it in the can. That's the most important thing, to get it in the can, so I can edit and at least have something to show people.

MAY 20, 1985

Went to see Tracy Camilla Johns in *Ceremonies in Dark Old Men*. It was good. I could tell it wasn't one of their best performances though, it was a little flat. Tracy was good in her role and she definitely has presence. I also saw another brother, Ruben Hudson, who could definitely read for Greer Childs. The guy is good plus he can act. Tracy says they have grown very close so he'll definitely be down. Then on top of that I ran into another one of Tracy's friends, a costume designer, his name is John Reefer. It was a good, good day yesterday.

JULY 6, 1985

Yesterday was the first official day of shooting. We shot the dog scene. It went well. Earl Smith, Brian Copeland and Erwin Wilson didn't show but we had backup. We shot it in the Bijou at NYU.[1] We have been hit by unexpected expenses—right now I can't worry about that. I pray to God that the $100s come in that we so desperately need.

I'm confident and I will be ready.

Today at the school we finalized the clothes people will wear. It really wasn't the time to work on scenes—we have done that. Monday we start to shoot and I'm getting ready, I can't even think about the money part. We have had seventeen or eighteen people pledge $100, but we are still waiting by the mailbox. I feel good.

Tomorrow we will look at the dance scene in its entirety. Then Monday morning we shoot. I do not foresee any big problems. It's a light day. Maybe transporting people will be a problem but it shouldn't be if we are coordinated.

Right now I'm gonna read the script again.

JULY 20, 1985

All praises due, at 7:40 P.M. the 20th of July in the year of our Lord 1985 we completed principal photography on *She's Gotta Have It*. That's it, done. The whole day was festive. Mr. Strawder, the owner of the Ferry Bank Restaurant, sent us three bottles of champagne. Monty had everybody fired up.

1 **NYU:** New York University

AUGUST 12, 1985

Wednesday morning I start to cut. I will cut six days a week. I'll take Sundays off to go watch football at Uncle Cliff's house. Working six days a week I should have a cut (rough) out by the beginning of October, from there it's on to a fine cut. Plus the pickup, reshoots, titles, opticals, cut in.

I should be jumping for joy, Cheryl Hill was my last chance. The reason I haven't jumped is because I haven't seen any money yet. There are about $20,000 in back salaries, loans to be paid. People are giving me to September then my phone is really gonna be ringing off the hook. I'm putting the answering machine on.

OCTOBER 16, 1985

Things are getting critical money-wise. My rent was due on October 1st. Cheryl Burr needs her $500. I owe the Black Filmmaker Foundation $500. I can't ask Mama for another cent. Everybody has been real understanding but patience is wearing thin. I have some other possible sources of money. Plus I have more money coming from First Run Features. Things look bleak right now but I can see the light at the end of the tunnel.

OCTOBER 22, 1985

I can't even cut the film in peace. Howard Funsch called today and said I had to come up with $1,000 by today or the negative was definitely being auctioned. I even had a three-way conference call with Kendall, but Funsch wouldn't budge. That was it. I made a desperation call to Nelson George who was just about to leave his house. THANK GOD FOR NELSON GEORGE. He came through like a champ. He and I went into the city to his American Express bank. He gave me $500 in cash and $500 in American Express traveler's checks. I'm at Du Art now waiting for Funsch. He went out to lunch. Nelson also gave me a list of high-powered people who might have the money. So he has really come through. THANK THE LORD. All praises due.

MARCH 20, 1986

Today is my 29th birthday. It was a furious day. Last night I screened *She's Gotta Have It* for Jean-Pierre Deleau and Olivier Jahon of the Cannes Film Festival. I didn't go to the screening—it's bad luck—so I left it up to Pamm Jackson. She took care of everything. After the screening they told her that we had been accepted. I talked to them in person and it's official, plus at the time we were the only film accepted. When I came back home I had a lot of birthday wishes on the answering machine. Olivier asked me to write a paragraph about the film for tomorrow before he leaves.

It might go something like this:

Today was my twenty-ninth birthday and I received a great present: My first feature film, *She's Gotta Have It,* was invited to Cannes for Director's Fortnight. I now (more than ever) believe that to make a film is one of the hardest tasks in life, and when you're an independent, it takes a miracle. I thank God and all who have been behind me from the start. Now for business: In the history of American cinema, too, too often black people have had to rely on Hollywood to tell our stories. I'm determined to change that even if it's in only a small way. We shouldn't have to rely on the Spielbergs[2] to define our existence. Blacks have to produce their own films, period.

Spike Lee March 20th, 1986. Brooklyn, New York, U.S.A.

APRIL 7, 1986

Last Thursday George Lucas[3] had his secretary call. He wants to see the film. I almost fell out of my chair. We tried to hook it up but it was to no avail. He'll have to wait till we come back from Cannes. It's official, *She's Gotta Have It* as of today is the only American independent film invited to Director's Fortnight. So that's a coup. ✳

2 **Spielbergs:** term refers to Steven Spielberg, a successful filmmaker, and others like him

3 **George Lucas:** successful movie director, producer, and screenwriter whose most notable work is *Star Wars*

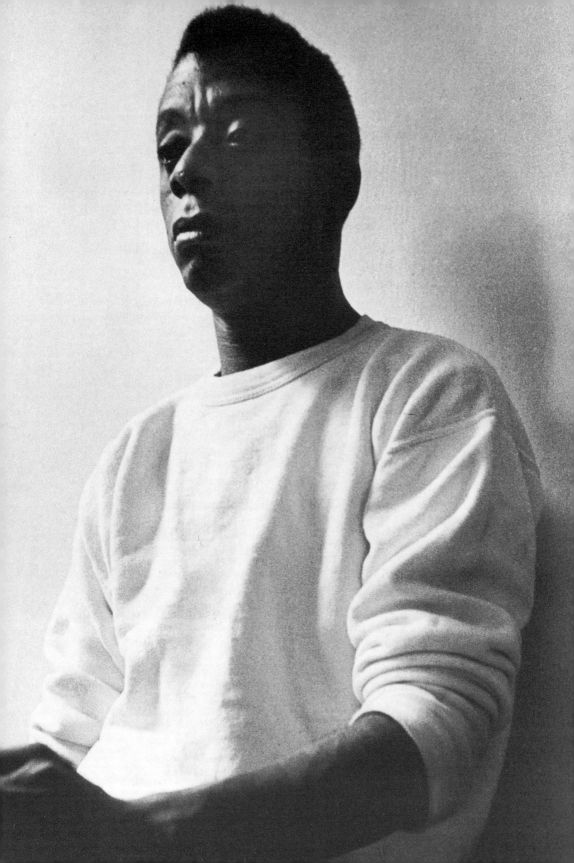

IF BLACK ENGLISH
ISN'T A LANGUAGE,
THEN TELL ME, WHAT IS?

James Baldwin

Born and raised in Harlem, James Baldwin (1924–87) is ranked among the most influential black authors in U.S. history. His novels, plays, and essays realistically demonstrate the effects of racism in the United States and abroad. The following excerpt from a 1979 article explains the origin and role of black English.

It goes without saying ... that language is ... a political instrument, means, and proof of power. It is the most vivid and crucial key to identity: It reveals the private identity, and connects one with, or divorces one from, the larger public, or communal identity. There have been, and are, times, and places, when to speak a certain language could be dangerous, even fatal. Or, one may speak the same language, but in such a way that one's antecedents are revealed, or (one hopes) hidden. This is true in France, and is absolutely true in England. The range (and reign) of accents on that damp little island make England coherent for the English and totally incomprehensible for everyone else. To open your mouth in England is (if I may use black English) to "put your business in the street": You have confessed your parents, your youth, your school, your salary, your self-esteem, and, alas, your future.

Now, I do not know what white Americans would sound like if there had never been any black people in the United States, but they would not sound the way they sound. *Jazz*, for example, is a very specific sexual term, as in *jazz me, baby*, but white people purified it into the Jazz Age. *Sock it to me*, which means, roughly, the same thing, has been adopted by Nathaniel Hawthorne's descendants with no qualms or hesitations at all, along with *let it all hang out* and *right on! Beat to his socks,* which was once the black's most total and despairing image of poverty, was transformed into a thing called the Beat Generation, which phenomenon was, largely, composed of *uptight,* middle-class white people, imitating poverty, trying to *get down,* to get *with it,* doing their *thing,* doing their despairing best to be funky, which we, the blacks, never dreamed of doing—we were *funky,* baby, like *funk* was going out of style.

Now, no one can eat his cake, and have it, too, and it is late in the day to attempt to penalize black people for having created a language that permits the nation its only glimpse of reality, a language without which the nation would be even more *whipped* than it is.

I say that this present skirmish is rooted in American history, and it is. Black English is the creation of the black diaspora. Blacks came to the United States chained to each other, but from different tribes: Neither could speak the other's language. If two black people, at that bitter hour of the world's history, had been able to speak to each other, the institution of chattel slavery[1] could never have lasted as long as it did. Subsequently, the slave was given, under the eye, and the gun, of his master, Congo Square,[2] and the Bible—or, in other words, and under these conditions, the slave began the formation of the black church, and it is within this unprecedented tabernacle that black English began to be formed. This was not, merely, as in the European example, the adoption of a foreign tongue, but an alchemy that transformed ancient elements into new language: *A language comes into existence by means of brutal necessity, and the rules of the language are dictated by what the language must convey.*

There was a moment, in time, and in this place, when my brother, or my mother, or my father, or my sister, had to convey to me, for example, the danger in which I was standing from the white man standing just behind me, and to convey this with a speed, and in a language, that the white man could not possibly understand, and that,

1 **chattel slavery:** the practice of treating African Americans as pieces of property owned by white Americans

2 **Congo Square:** one of the few places in New Orleans where African Americans were allowed to gather socially

indeed, he cannot understand, until today. He cannot afford to understand it. This understanding would reveal to him too much about himself, and smash that mirror before which he has been frozen for so long.

Now, if this passion, this skill, this (to quote Toni Morrison[3]) "sheer intelligence," this incredible music, the mighty achievement of having brought a people utterly unknown to, or despised by "history"—to have brought this people to their present, troubled, troubling, and unassailable and unanswerable place—if this absolutely unprecedented journey does not indicate that black English is a language, I am curious to know what definition of language is to be trusted.

A people at the center of the Western world, and in the midst of so hostile a population, has not endured and transcended by means of what is patronizingly called a "dialect." We, the blacks, are in trouble, certainly, but we are not doomed, and we are not inarticulate because we are not compelled to defend a morality that we know to be a lie.

The brutal truth is that the bulk of the white people in America never had any interest in educating black people, except as this could serve white purposes. It is not the black child's language that is in question, it is not his language that is despised: It is his experience. A child cannot be taught by anyone who despises him, and a child cannot afford to be fooled. A child cannot be taught by anyone whose demand, essentially, is that the child repudiate his experience, and all that gives him sustenance, and enter a limbo in which he will no longer be black, and in which he knows that he can never become white. Black people have lost too many black children that way.

And, after all, finally, in a country with standards so untrustworthy, a country that makes heroes of so many criminal mediocrities, a country unable to face why so many of the nonwhite are in prison, or on the needle, or standing, futureless, in the streets—it may very well be that both the child, and his elder, have concluded that they have nothing whatever to learn from the people of a country that has managed to learn so little. ✳

---

3 **Toni Morrison:** contemporary author; first African American female to win the Nobel Prize

IN SEARCH OF
ZORA NEALE HURSTON

Alice Walker

Zora Neale Hurston (1903–1959) is one of the most significant writers
of the Harlem Renaissance. A native of Eatonville, Florida, Hurston
wrote vividly about her hometown in her novels. She also used
her travels to Harlem as a basis for her writing. Although she saw little
national literary success in her lifetime, critics have since gained
a new appreciation for her work.

In this piece, contemporary novelist Alice Walker writes candidly
about her search for more information on the life of an author
she greatly admired.

On August 15, 1973, I wake up just as the plane is lowering over Sanford, Florida, which means I am also looking down on Eatonville, Zora Neale Hurston's birthplace. I recognize it from Zora's description in *Mules and Men*: "the city of five lakes, three croquet courts, three hundred brown skins, three hundred good swimmers, plenty guavas,[1] two schools, and no jailhouse." Of course I cannot see the guavas, but five lakes are still there, and it is the lakes I count as the plane prepares to land in Orlando.

From the air, Florida looks completely flat, and as we near the ground this impression does not change. This is the first time I have seen the interior of the state, which Zora wrote about so well, but there are the acres of orange groves, the sand, mangrove trees, and scrub pine that I know from her books. Getting off the plane I walk through

---

1 **guavas:** shrubby trees with pink or yellow tropical fruit

Alice Walker at her desk

the hot moist air of midday into the tacky but air-conditioned airport. I search for Charlotte Hunt, my companion on the Zora Hurston expedition. She lives in Winter Park, Florida, very near Eatonville, and is writing her graduate dissertation on Zora. I see her waving—a large pleasant-faced white woman in dark glasses. We have written to each other for several weeks, swapping our latest finds (mostly hers) on Zora, and trying to make sense out of the mass of information obtained (often erroneous or simply confusing) from Zora herself—through her stories and autobiography—and from people who wrote about her.

Eatonville has lived for such a long time in my imagination that I can hardly believe it will be found existing in its own right. But after 20 minutes on the expressway, Charlotte turns off and I see a small settlement of houses and stores set with no particular pattern in the sandy soil off the road. We stop in front of a neat gray building that has two fascinating signs: Eatonville Post Office and Eatonville City Hall.

Inside the Eatonville City Hall half of the building, a slender, dark brown-skin woman sits looking through letters on a desk. When she hears we are searching for anyone who might have known Zora Neale Hurston, she leans back in thought. Because I don't wish to inspire foot-dragging in people who might know something about Zora they're not sure they should tell, I have decided on a simple, but I feel profoundly useful, lie.

"I am Miss Hurston's niece," I prompt the young woman, who brings her head down with a smile.

"I think Mrs. Moseley is about the only one still living who might remember her," she says.

"Do you mean *Mathilda* Moseley, the woman who tells those 'woman-is-smarter-than-man' lies in Zora's book?"

"Yes," says the young woman. "Mrs. Moseley is real old now, of course. But this time of day, she would be at home."

I stand at the counter looking down on her, the first Eatonville resident I have spoken to. Because of Zora's books, I feel I know something about her; at least I know what the town she grew up in was like years before she was born.

"Tell me something," I say, "do the schools teach Zora's books here?"

"No," she says, "they don't. I don't think most people know anything about Zora Neale Hurston, or know about any of the great things she did. She was a fine lady. I've read all of her books myself, but I don't think many other folks in Eatonville have."

"Many of the church people around here, as I understand it," says Charlotte in a murmured aside, "thought Zora was pretty loose. I don't think they appreciated her writing about them."

"Well," I say to the young woman, "thank you for your help." She clarifies her directions to Mrs. Moseley's house and smiles as Charlotte and I turn to go.

▲ ● ▲

The letter to *Harper's* does not expose a publisher's rejection of an unknown masterpiece, but it does reveal how the bright promise of the Harlem Renaissance deteriorated for many of the writers who shared in its exuberance. It also indicates the personal tragedy of Zora Neale Hurston: Barnard graduate, author of four novels, two books of folklore, one volume of autobiography, the most important collector of Afro-American folklore in America, reduced by poverty and circumstance to seek a publisher by unsolicited mail.

—Robert Hemenway

▲ • ▲

Zora Hurston was born in 1901, 1902, or 1903—depending on how old she felt herself to be at the time someone asked.

—Librarian, Beinecke Library, Yale University

▲ • ▲

The Moseley house is small and white and snug, its tiny yard nearly swallowed up by oleanders and hibiscus bushes. Charlotte and I knock on the door. I call out. But there is no answer. This strikes us as peculiar. We have had time to figure out an age for Mrs. Moseley—not dates or a number, just old. I am thinking of a quivery, bedridden invalid when we hear the car. We look behind us to see an old black-and-white Buick—paint peeling and grillwork rusty—pulling into the drive. A neat old lady in a purple dress and white hair is straining at the wheel. She is frowning because Charlotte's car is in the way.

Mrs. Moseley looks at us suspiciously. "Yes, I knew Zora Neale," she says, unsmilingly and with a rather cold stare at Charlotte (who I imagine feels very *white* at that moment), "but that was a long time ago, and I don't want to talk about it."

"Yes ma'am," I murmur, bringing all my sympathy to bear on the situation.

"Not only that," Mrs. Moseley continues, "I've been sick. Been in the hospital for an operation. Ruptured artery. The doctors didn't believe I was going to live, but you see me alive, don't you?"

"Looking well, too," I comment.

Mrs. Moseley is out of her car. A thin, sprightly woman with nice gold-studded false teeth, uppers and lowers. I like her because she stands there *straight* beside her car, with a hand on her hip and her straw pocketbook on her arm. She wears white T-strap shoes with heels that show off her well-shaped legs.

"I'm eighty-two years old, you know," she says. "And I just can't remember things the way I used to. Anyhow, Zora Neale left here to go to school and she never really came back to live. She'd come here for material for her books, but that was all. She spent most of her time down in South Florida."

"You know, Mrs. Moseley, I saw your name in one of Zora's books."

Zora interviewing folk musicians, 1935

"You did?" She looks at me with only slightly more interest. "I read some of her books a long time ago, but then people got to borrowing and borrowing and they borrowed them all away."

"I could send you a copy of everything that's been reprinted," I offer. "Would you like me to do that?"

"No," says Mrs. Moseley promptly. "I don't read much any more. Besides, all that was *so* long ago . . ."

Charlotte and I settle back against the car in the sun. Mrs. Moseley tells us at length and with exact recall every step in her recent operation, ending with: "What those doctors didn't know—when they were expecting me to die (and they didn't even think I'd live long enough for them to have to take out my stitches!)—is that Jesus is the best doctor, and if *He* says for you to get well, that's all that counts."

With this philosophy, Charlotte and I murmur quick assent: being Southerners and church bred, we have heard that belief before. But what we learn from Mrs. Moseley is that she does not remember much beyond the year 1938. She shows us a picture of her father and mother and says that her father was Joe Clarke's brother. Joe Clarke, as every Zora Hurston reader knows, was the first mayor of Eatonville; his fictional counterpart is Jody Starks of *Their Eyes Were Watching*

God. We also get directions to where Joe Clarke's store *was*—where Club Eaton is now. Club Eaton, a long orange-beige nightspot we had seen on the main road, is apparently famous for the good times in it regularly had by all. It is, perhaps, the modern equivalent of the store porch, where all the men of Zora's childhood came to tell "lies," that is, black folktales, that were "made and used on the spot," to take a line from Zora. As for Zora's exact birthplace, Mrs. Moseley has no idea.

After I have commented on the healthy growth of her hibiscus bushes, she becomes more talkative. She mentions how much she *loved* to dance, when she was a young woman, and talks about how good her husband was. When he was alive, she says, she was completely happy because he allowed her to be completely free. "I was so free I had to pinch myself sometimes to tell if I was a married woman."

Relaxed now, she tells us about going to school with Zora. "Zora and I went to the same school. It's called Hungerford High now. It *was* only to the eighth grade. But our teachers were so good that by the time you left you knew college subjects. When I went to Morris Brown in Atlanta, the teachers there were just teaching me the same things I had already learned right in Eatonville. I wrote Mama and told her I was going to come home and help her with her babies. I wasn't learning anything new."

"Tell me something, Mrs. Moseley," I ask, "why do you suppose Zora was against integration? I read somewhere that she was against school desegregation because she felt it was an insult to black teachers."

"Oh, one of them [white people] came around asking me about integration. One day I was doing my shopping. I heard 'em over there talking about it in the store, about the schools. And I got on out of the way because I knew if they asked me, they wouldn't like what I was going to tell 'em. But they came up and asked me anyhow. 'What do you think about this integration?' one of them said. I acted like I thought I had heard wrong. 'You're asking *me* what *I* think about integration?' I said. 'Well, as you can see I'm just an old colored woman'—I was seventy-five or seventy-six then—'and this is the first time anybody ever asked me about integration. And nobody asked my grandmother what she thought, either, but her daddy was one of you all.'" Mrs. Moseley seems satisfied with this memory of her rejoinder.

She looks at Charlotte. "I have the blood of three races in my veins," she says belligerently, "white, black, and Indian, and nobody asked me *anything* before."

"Do you think living in Eatonville made integration less appealing to you?"

"Well, I can tell you this: I have lived in Eatonville all my life, and I've been in the governing of this town. I've been everything but Mayor and I've been *assistant* Mayor. Eatonville was and is an all-black town. We have our own police department, post office, and town hall. Our own school and good teachers. Do I need integration?

"They took over Goldsboro, because the black people who lived there never incorporated, like we did. And now I don't even know if any black folks live there. They built big houses up there around the lakes. But we didn't let that happen in Eatonville, and we don't sell land to just anybody. And you see, we're still here."

When we leave, Mrs. Moseley is standing by her car, waving. I think of the letter Roy Wilkins wrote to a black newspaper blasting Zora Neale for her lack of enthusiasm about the integration of schools. I wonder if he knew the experience of Eatonville she was coming from. Not many black people in America have come from a self-contained, all-black community where loyalty and unity are taken for granted. A place where black pride is nothing new.

There is, however, one thing Mrs. Moseley said that bothered me.

"Tell me, Mrs. Moseley," I had asked, "why is it that thirteen years after Zora's death, no marker has been put on her grave?"

And Mrs. Moseley answered: "The reason she doesn't have a stone is because she wasn't buried here. She was buried down in South Florida somewhere. I don't think anybody really knew where she was."

▲ ● ▲

Only to reach a wider audience, need she ever write books—because she is a perfect book of entertainment in herself. In her youth she was always getting scholarships and things from wealthy white people, some of whom simply paid her just to sit around and represent the Negro race for them, she did it in such a racy fashion. She was full of sidesplitting anecdotes, humorous tales, and tragicomic stories, remembered out of her life in the South as a daughter of a traveling minister of God. She could make you laugh one minute and cry the next. To many of her white friends, no doubt, she was a perfect "darkie," in the nice meaning they give the term—that is, a naïve, childlike, sweet, humorous, and highly colored Negro.

But Miss Hurston was clever, too—a student who didn't let college give her a broad "a" and who had great scorn for all pretensions, academic or otherwise. That is why she was such a fine folklore collector, able to go among the people and never act as if she had been to school at all. Almost nobody else could stop the average Harlemite on Lenox Avenue and measure his head with a strange-looking, anthropological device and not be bawled out for the attempt, except Zora, who used to stop anyone whose head looked interesting, and measure it.

—Langston Hughes, *The Big Sea* (Knopf)

▲ ● ▲

What does it matter what white folks must have thought about her?
—Student, "Black Women Writers" class, Wellesley College

▲ ● ▲

Mrs. Sarah Peek Patterson is a handsome, red-haired woman in her late forties, wearing orange slacks and gold earrings. She is the director of Lee-Peek Mortuary in Fort Pierce, the establishment that handled Zora's burial. Unlike most black funeral homes in Southern towns that sit like palaces among the general poverty, Lee-Peek has a run-down, *small* look. Perhaps this is because it is painted purple and white, as are its Cadillac chariots. These colors do not age well. The rooms are cluttered and grimy, and the bathroom is a tiny, stale-smelling prison, with a bottle of black hair dye (apparently used to touch up the hair of the corpses) dripping into the face bowl. Two pine burial boxes are resting in the bathtub.

Mrs. Patterson herself is pleasant and helpful.

"As I told you over the phone, Mrs. Patterson," I begin, shaking her hand and looking into her penny-brown eyes, "I am Zora Neale Hurston's niece, and I would like to have a marker put on her grave. You said, when I called you last week, that you could tell me where the grave is."

By this time I am, of course, completely into being Zora's niece, and the lie comes with perfect naturalness to my lips. Besides, as far as I'm concerned, she *is* my aunt—and that of all black people as well.

"She was buried in 1960," exclaims Mrs. Patterson. "That was when my father was running this funeral home. He's sick now or I'd let you talk to him. But I know where she's buried. She's in the old cemetery, the Garden of the Heavenly Rest, on Seventeenth Street. Just when you go in the gate, there's a circle, and she's buried right in the middle of it. Hers is the only grave in that circle—because people don't bury in that cemetery any more."

She turns to a stocky, black-skinned woman in her thirties, wearing a green polo shirt and white jeans cut off at the knee. "This lady will show you where it is," she says.

"I can't tell you how much I appreciate this," I say to Mrs. Patterson, as I rise to go. "And could you tell me something else? You see, I never met my aunt. When she died, I was still a junior in high school. But could you tell me what she died of, and what kind of funeral she had?"

"I don't know exactly what she died of," Mrs. Patterson says. "I know she didn't have any money. Folks took up a collection to bury her. . . . I believe she died of malnutrition."

"*Malnutrition?*"

Outside, in the blistering sun, I lean my head against Charlotte's even more blistering cartop. The sting of the hot metal only intensifies my anger. "*Malnutrition*," I manage to mutter. "Hell, our condition hasn't changed *any* since Phillis Wheatley's[2] time. *She* died of malnutrition!"

"Really?" says Charlotte, "I didn't know that."

▲ ● ▲

One cannot overemphasize the extent of her commitment. It was so great that her marriage in the spring of 1927 to Herbert Sheen was short-lived. Although divorce did not come officially until 1931, the two separated amicably after only a few months, Hurston to continue her collecting, Sheen to attend Medical School. Hurston never married again.

—Robert Hemenway

2 **Phillis Wheatley:** black American poet, 1753?-1784

▲ ● ▲

"What is your name?" I ask the woman who has climbed into the back seat.

"Rosalee," she says. She has a rough, pleasant voice, as if she is a singer who also smokes a lot. She is homely, and has an air of ready indifference.

"Another woman came by here wanting to see the grave," she says, lighting up a cigarette. "She was a little short, dumpy white lady from one of these Florida schools. Orlando or Daytona. But let me tell you something before we gets started. All I know is where the cemetery is. I don't know one thing about that grave. You better go back in and ask her to draw you a map."

A few moments later, with Mrs. Patterson's diagram of where the grave is, we head for the cemetery.

We drive past blocks of small, pastel-colored houses and turn right onto 17th Street. At the very end, we reach a tall curving gate, with the words "Garden of the Heavenly Rest" fading into the stone. I expected, from Mrs. Patterson's small drawing, to find a small circle—which would have placed Zora's grave five or ten paces from the road. But the "circle" is over an acre large and looks more like an abandoned field. Tall weeds choke the dirt road and scrape against the sides of the car. It doesn't help either that I step out into an active anthill.

"I don't know about y'all," I say, "but I don't even believe this." I am used to the haphazard cemetery-keeping that is traditional in most Southern black communities, but this neglect is staggering. As far I as can see there is nothing but bushes and weeds, some as tall as my waist. One grave is near the road, and Charlotte elects to investigate it. It is fairly clean, and belongs to someone who died in 1963.

Rosalee and I plunge into the weeds; I pull my long dress up to my hips. The weeds scratch my knees, and the insects have a feast. Looking back, I see Charlotte standing resolutely near the road.

"Aren't you coming?" I call.

"No," she calls back. "I'm from these parts and I know what's out there." She means snakes.

My whole life and the people I love flash melodramatically before my eyes. Rosalee is a few yards to my right.

"How're you going to find anything out here?" she asks. And I stand still a few seconds, looking at the weeds. Some of them are quite pretty, with tiny yellow flowers. They are thick and healthy, but dead weeds under them have formed a thick gray carpet on the ground. A snake could be lying six inches from my big toe and I wouldn't see it. We move slowly, very slowly, our eyes alert, our legs trembly. It is hard to tell where the center of the circle is since the circle is not really round, but more like half of something round. There are things crackling and hissing in the grass. Sandspurs[3] are sticking to the inside of my skirt. Sand and ants cover my feet. I look toward the road and notice that there are, indeed two large curving stones, making an entrance and exit to the cemetery. I take my bearings from them and try to navigate to exact center. But the center of anything can be very large, and a grave is not a pinpoint. Finding the grave seems positively hopeless. There is only one thing to do:

Zora Neale Hurston at the Federal Writers' Project exhibit, 1938

"Zora!" I yell, as loud as I can (causing Rosalee to jump), "are you out here?"

"If she is, I sho hope she don't answer you. If she do, I'm gone."

"Zora!" I call again. "I'm here. Are you?"

"If she is," grumbles Rosalee, "I hope she'll keep it to herself."

"Zora!" Then I start fussing with her. "I hope you don't think I'm going to stand out here all day, with these snakes watching me and these ants having a field day. In fact, I'm going to call you just one or two more times." On a clump of dried grass, near a small bushy tree, my eye falls on one of the largest bugs I have ever seen. It is on its back, and is as large as three of my fingers. I walk toward it, and yell "Zo-ra!" and my foot sinks into a hole. I look down. I am standing in a sunken rectangle that is about six feet long and about three or four feet wide. I look up to see where the two gates are.

3 **sandspurs:** burrs produced by certain types of grasses

"Well," I say, "this is the center, or approximately anyhow. It's also the only sunken spot we've found. Doesn't this look like a grave to you?"

"For the sake of not going no farther through these bushes," Rosalee growls, "yes, it do."

"Wait a minute," I say, "I have to look around some more to be sure this is the only spot that resembles a grave. But you don't have to come."

Rosalee smiles—a grin, really—beautiful and tough.

"Naw," she says, "I feels sorry for you. If one of these snakes got ahold of you out here by yourself I'd feel real bad." She laughs. "I done come this far, I'll go on with you."

"Thank you, Rosalee," I say. "Zora thanks you too."

"Just as long as she don't try to tell me in person," she says, and together we walk down the field.

▲ ● ▲

The gusto and flavor of Zora Neal[e] Hurston's stoytelling, for example, long before the yarns were published in *"Mules and Men"* and other books, became a local legend which might. . . have spread further under different conditions. A tiny shift in the center of gravity could have made them best-sellers.

—Arna Bontemps, *Personals* (Paul Bremen, Ltd., London; 1963)

▲ ● ▲

Bitter over the rejection of her folklore's value, especially in the black community, frustrated by what she felt was her failure to convert the Afro-American world view into the forms of prose fiction, Hurston finally gave up.

—Robert Hemenway

▲ ● ▲

When Charlotte and I drive up to the Merritt Monument Company, I immediately see the headstone I want. "How much is this one?" I ask the young woman in charge, pointing to a tall black stone. It looks as majestic as Zora herself must have been when she was learning voodoo[4] from those root doctors down in New Orleans.

4 **voodoo:** a religion derived from the African worship of many gods

"Oh, *that* one," she says, "that's our finest. That's Ebony Mist."

"Well, how much is it?"

"I don't know. But wait," she says, looking around in relief, "here comes somebody who'll know."

A small, sunburned man with squinty green eyes comes up. He must be the engraver, I think, because his eyes are contracted into slits, as if he has been keeping stone dust out of them for years.

"That's Ebony Mist," he says. "That's our best."

"How much is it?" I ask, beginning to realize I probably *can't* afford it.

He gives me a price that would feed a dozen Sahelian[5] drought victims for three years. I realize I must honor the dead, but between the dead great and the living starving, there is no choice.

"I have a lot of letters to be engraved," I say, standing by the plain gray marker I have chosen. It is pale and ordinary, not at all like Zora, and makes me momentarily angry that I am not rich.

We go into his office and I hand him a sheet of paper that has:

ZORA NEALE HURSTON
"A GENIUS OF THE SOUTH"
NOVELIST, FOLKLORIST,
ANTHROPOLOGIST
1901–1960

"A genius of the South" is from one of Jean Toomer's poems.

"Where is the grave?" the monument man asks. "If it's in a new cemetery, the stone has to be flat."

"Well, it's not a new cemetery and Zora—my aunt—doesn't need anything flat because with the weeds out there, you'd never be able to see it. You'll have to go out there with me."

He grunts.

"And take a long pole and 'sound' the spot," I add. "Because there's no way of telling it's a grave, except that it's sunken."

"Well," he says, after taking my money and writing up a receipt, in the full awareness that he's the only monument dealer for miles, "you take this flag" (he hands me a four-foot-long pole with a red-metal

---

5 **Sahelian:** people from the desert region south of the Sahara in Africa

marker on top) "and take it out to the cemetery and put it where you think the grave is. It'll take us about three weeks to get the stone out there."

I wonder if he knows he is sending me to another confrontation with the snakes. He probably does. Charlotte has told me she will cut my leg and suck out the blood, if I am bit.

"At least send me a photograph when it's done, won't you?"

He says he will.

▲ ● ▲

Hurston's return to her folklore-collecting in December of 1927 was made possible by Mrs. R. Osgood Mason, an elderly white patron of the arts, who at various times also helped Langston Hughes, Alain Locke, Richmond Barthe, and Miguel Covarrubias. Hurston apparently came to her attention through the intercession of Locke, who frequently served as a kind of liaison between the young black talent and Mrs. Mason. The entire relationship between this woman and the Harlem Renaissance deserves extended study, for it represents much of the ambiguity involved in white patronage of black artists. All her artists were instructed to call her "Godmother"; there was a decided emphasis on the "primitive" aspects of black culture, apparently a holdover from Mrs. Mason's interest in the Plains Indians. In Hurston's case there were special restrictions imposed by her patron: although she was to be paid a handsome salary for her folklore-collecting, she was to limit her correspondence and publish nothing of her research without prior approval.

—Robert Hemenway

▲ ● ▲

You have to read the chapters Zora left out of her autobiography.

—Student, Special Collections Room, Beinecke Library, Yale University

▲ ● ▲

Dr. Benton, a friend of Zora's and a practicing M.D. in Fort Pierce, is one of those old, good-looking men whom I always have trouble not liking. (It no longer bothers me that I may be constantly searching for father figures; by this time, I have found several and dearly enjoyed knowing them all.) He is shrewd, with steady brown eyes under hair that is almost white. He is probably in his seventies, but doesn't look it. He carries himself with dignity, and has cause to be proud of the new clinic where he now practices medicine. His nurse looks at us with suspicion, but Dr. Benton's eyes have the penetration of a scalpel cutting through skin. I guess right away that if he knows anything at all about Zora Hurston, he will not believe I am her niece. "Eatonville?" Dr. Benton says, leaning forward in his chair, looking first at me, then at Charlotte. "Yes, I know Eatonville, I grew up not far from there. I knew the whole bunch of Zora's family." (He looks at the shape of my cheekbones, the size of my eyes, and the nappiness of my hair.) "I knew her daddy. The old man. He was a hardworking, Christian man. Did the best he could for his family. He was the mayor of Eatonville for a while, you know.

"My father was the mayor of Goldsboro. You probably never heard of it. It never incorporated like Eatonville did, and has just about disappeared. But Eatonville is still all-black."

He pauses and looks at me. "And you're Zora's niece," he says wonderingly.

"Well," I say with shy dignity, yet with some tinge, I hope, of a 19th-century blush, "I'm illegitimate. That's why I never knew Aunt Zora."

I love him for the way he comes to my rescue. "You're *not* illegitimate!" he cries, his eyes resting on me fondly. "All of us are God's children! Don't you even *think* such a thing!"

And I hate myself for lying to him. Still, I ask myself, would I have gotten this far toward getting the headstone and finding out about Zora Hurston's last days without telling my lie? Actually, I probably would have. But I don't like taking chances that could get me stranded in Central Florida.

"Zora didn't get along with her family. I don't know why. Did you read her autobiography, *Dust Tracks on a Road*?"

"Yes, I did," I say. "It pained me to see Zora pretending to be naive and grateful about the old white 'Godmother' who helped finance her research, but I loved the part where she ran off from home after falling out with her brother's wife."

Dr. Benton nodded. "When she got sick, I tried to get her to go back to her family, but she refused. There wasn't any real hatred; they just never had gotten along and Zora wouldn't go to them. She didn't want to go to the county home, either, but she had to, because she couldn't do a thing for herself."

"I was surprised to learn she died of malnutrition."

Dr. Benton seems startled. "Zora *didn't* die of malnutrition," he says indignantly. "Where did you get that story from? She had a stroke and she died in the welfare home." He seems peculiarly upset, distressed, but sits back reflectively in his chair: "She was an incredible woman," he muses. "Sometimes when I closed my office, I'd go by her house and just talk to her for an hour or two. She was a well-read, well-traveled woman and always had her own ideas about what was going on . . ."

"I never knew her, you know. Only some of Carl Van Vechten's photographs and some newspaper photographs. . . .What did she look like?"

"When I knew her, in the fifties, she was a big woman, *erect*. Not quite as light as I am [Dr. Benton is dark beige], and about five foot, seven inches, and she weighed about two hundred pounds. Probably more. She . . ."

"What! Zora was *fat*! She wasn't, in Van Vechten's pictures!"

"Zora loved to eat," Dr. Benton says complacently. "She could sit down with a mound of ice cream and just eat and talk till it was all gone."

While Dr. Benton is talking, I recall that the Van Vechten pictures were taken when Zora was still a young woman. In them she appears tall, tan, and healthy. In later newspaper photographs—when she was in her forties—I remembered that she seemed heavier and several shades lighter. I reasoned that the earlier photographs were taken while she was busy collecting folklore materials in the hot Florida sun.

"She had high blood pressure. Her health wasn't good. . . . She used to live in one of my houses—on School Court Street. It's a block house . . . I don't recall the number. But my wife and I used to invite her over to the house for dinner. *She always ate well*," he says emphatically.

"That's comforting to know," I say, wondering where Zora ate when she wasn't with the Bentons.

"Sometimes she would run out of groceries—after she got sick—and she'd call me. 'Come over here and see 'bout me,' she'd say. And I'd take her shopping and buy her groceries.

"She was always studying. Her mind—before the stroke—just worked all the time. She was always going somewhere, too. She once went to Honduras[6] to study something. And when she died, she was working on that book about Herod the Great.[7] She was so intelligent! And really had perfect expressions. Her English was beautiful." (I suspect this is a clever way to let me know Zora herself didn't speak in the "black English" her characters used.)

"I used to read all of her books," Dr. Benton continues, "but it was a long time ago. I remember one about . . . it was called, I think, 'The Children of God' [*Their Eyes Were Watching God*], and I remember Janie and Teapot [Teacake] and the mad dog riding on the cow in that hurricane and bit old Teapot on the cheek . . ."

I am delighted that he remembers even this much of the story, even if the names are wrong, but seeing his affection for Zora I feel I must ask him about her burial. "Did she *really* have a pauper's funeral?"[8]

"She *didn't* have a pauper's funeral!" he says with great heat. "Everybody around here *loved* Zora."

"We just came back from ordering a headstone," I say quietly, because he is an old man and the color is coming and going on his face, "but to tell the truth, I can't be positive what I found is the grave. All I know is the spot I found was the only grave-size hole in the area."

"I remember it wasn't near the road," says Dr. Benton, more calmly. "Some other lady came by here and we went out looking for the grave and I took a long iron stick and poked all over that part of the cemetery but we didn't find anything. She took some pictures of the general area. Do the weeds still come up to your knees?"

"And beyond," I murmur. This time there isn't any doubt. Dr. Benton feels ashamed.

As he walks us to our car, he continues to talk about Zora. "She couldn't really write much near the end. She had the stroke and it left her weak; her mind was affected. She couldn't think about anything for long.

"She came here from Daytona, I think. She owned a house-boat over there. When she came here, she sold it. She lived on that money,

6 **Honduras:** a country in Central America

7 **Herod the Great:** a Roman king from biblical times

8 **pauper's funeral:** a simple burial for those who have no one able to pay for it

then she worked as a maid—for an article on maids she was writing—and she worked for the *Chronicle* writing the horoscope column.

"I think black people here in Florida got mad at her because she was for some politician they were against. She said this politician *built* schools for blacks while the one they wanted just talked about it. And although Zora wasn't egotistical, what she thought, she thought; and generally what she thought, she said."

When we leave Dr. Benton's office, I realize I have missed my plane back home to Jackson, Mississippi. That being so, Charlotte and I decide to find the house Zora lived in before she was taken to the county welfare home to die. From among her many notes, Charlotte locates a letter of Zora's she has copied that carries the address: 1734 School Court Street. We ask several people for directions. Finally, two old gentlemen in a dusty gray Plymouth offer to lead us there. School Court Street is not paved, and the road is full of mud puddles. It is dismal and squalid, redeemed only by the brightness of the late afternoon sun. Now I can understand what a "block" house is. It is a house shaped like a block, for one thing, surrounded by others just like it. Some houses are blue and some are green or yellow. Zora's is light green. They are tiny—about 50 by 50 feet, squatty with flat roofs. The house Zora lived in looks worse than the others, but that is its only distinction. It also has three ragged and dirty children sitting on the steps.

"Is this where y'all live?" I ask, aiming my camera.

"No ma'am," they say in unison, looking at me earnestly. "We live over yonder. This Miss So-and-So's house; but she in the horspital."

We chatter inconsequentially while I take more pictures. A car drives up with a young black couple in it. They scowl fiercely at Charlotte and don't look at me with friendliness, either. They get out and stand in their doorway across the street. I go up to them to explain. "Did you know Zora Hurston used to live right across from you?" I ask.

"Who?" They stare at my blankly, then become curiously attentive, as if they think I made the name up. They are both Afro-ed[9] and he is somberly dashiki-ed.[10]

I suddenly feel frail and exhausted. "It's too long a story," I say, "but

9 **Afro-ed:** having a tightly-curled hairstyle kept in a full, evenly rounded shape
10 **dashiki-ed:** wearing loose, brightly colored African clothing

Zora Neale Hurston (center) and friends, probably in Fort Pierce, Florida, ca. 1958–59

tell me something, is there anybody on this street who's lived here for more than thirteen years?"

"That old man down there," the young man says, pointing. Sure enough, there is a man sitting on his steps three houses down. He has graying hair and is very neat, but there is a weakness about him. He reminds me of Mrs. Turner's husband in *Their Eyes Were Watching God*. He's rather "vanishing"-looking, as if his features have been sanded down. In the old days, before black was beautiful, he was probably considered attractive, because he has wavy hair and light-brown skin; but now, well, light skin has ceased to be its own reward.

After the preliminaries, there is only one thing I want to know: "Tell me something," I begin, looking down at Zora's house, "did Zora like flowers?"

He looks at me queerly. "As a matter of fact," he says, looking regretfully at the bare, rough yard that surrounds her former house, "she was crazy about them. And she was a great gardener. She loved azaleas, and that running and blooming vine [morning glories], and she really loved that night-smelling flower [gardenia]. She kept a vegetable garden year-round, too. She raised collards and tomatoes and things like that.

"Everyone in this community thought well of Miss Hurston. When she died, people all up and down this street took up a collection for her burial. We put her away nice."

"Why didn't somebody put up a headstone?"

"Well, you know, one was never requested. Her and her family didn't get along. They didn't even come to the funeral."

"And did she live down there by herself?"

"Yes, until they took her away. She lived with—just her and her companion, Sport."

My ears perked up. "Who?"

"Sport, you know, her dog. He was her only companion. He was a big brown-and-white dog."

When I walk back to the car, Charlotte is talking to the young couple on their porch. They are relaxed and smiling.

"I told them about the famous lady who used to live across the street from them," says Charlotte as we drive off. "Of course they had no idea Zora ever lived, let alone that she lived across the street. I think I'll send some of her books to them."

"That's real kind of you," I say.

▲ ● ▲

I am not tragically colored. There is no great sorrow dammed up in my soul, nor lurking behind my eyes. I do not mind at all. I do not belong to the sobbing school of Negrohood who hold that nature somehow has given them a lowdown dirty deal and whose feelings are all hurt about it. . . . No, I do not weep at the world—I am too busy sharpening my oyster knife.

—Zora Neale Hurston, "How It Feels to Be Colored Me"
World Tomorrow 1928

▲ ● ▲

There are times—and finding Zora Hurston's grave was one of them—when normal responses of grief, horror, and so on, do not make sense because they bear no real relation to the depth of the emotion one feels. It was impossible for me to cry when I saw the field full of weeds where Zora is. Partly this is because I have come to know Zora through her books and she was not a teary sort of person herself; but partly, too, it is because there is a point at which even grief feels absurd. And at this point, laughter gushes up to retrieve sanity.

It is only later, when the pain is not so direct a threat to one's own existence that what was learned in that moment of comical lunacy is understood. Such moments rob us of both youth and vanity. But perhaps they are also times when greater disciplines are born. ✳

Gravestone placed by Alice Walker in the
Garden of the Heavenly Rest, 1973

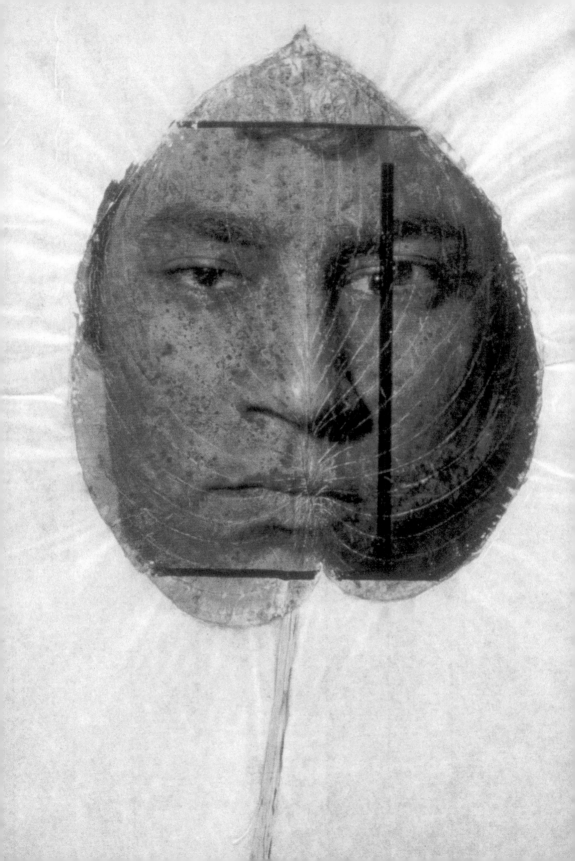

THERE'S A
HARLEM RENAISSANCE
IN MY HEAD

Maurice E. Duhon, Jr., age 17

The trombones slap me in the face with their high-life beats, and the piano's glamorous tunes tap me on my shoulder and whisper in my ear. As I look down into the Juke-Joint from my bedroom floor, rotted house, rotted life, plain rotten seems forgotten as the music plays and the beats go down to the rhythm of my heart's pound. There's a Harlem Renaissance in my head, there's a Harlem Renaissance in my head.

Through the floor a light, where the music roared, overtakes the darkness that surrounds me as I look through this floorboard. I can see the hoppin' and a dancin' and the suave men a prancin' around the young ladies who stand stunning on the floor. . .

The music stops, the poet stands up, and with each turn of the page, his mind's thoughts he will emancipate and everybody in the room he will captivate. His pen his only weapon with which injustice he must eradicate. As I look down into the Juke-Joint from my bedroom floor, rotted house, rotted life, plain rotten seems forgotten as the music plays and the beats go down to the rhythm of my thoughts' pound. There's a Harlem Renaissance in my head.

Let your ink run rampant, Langston Hughes. Let your fingers tickle the ivories forever, Duke. At every moment history being made in my own personal Juke-Joint. I lean my ears to hear even closer and find my mind in a past tense, opening my eyes to see beauty, but surrounded by pure silence. There's a Harlem Renaissance in my head, a Harlem Renaissance in my head. ✳

IAN I
1993
Accra Shepp

RESPONDING TO CLUSTER FOUR

Thinking Skill SYNTHESIZING

1. The other clusters in this book are introduced by a question that is meant to help readers focus their thinking about the selections. What do you think the question for Cluster Four should be?

2. How do you think the selections in this cluster should be taught? Demonstrate your ideas by joining with your classmates to: create discussion questions, lead discussions about the selections, develop vocabulary activities, and/or prepare a cluster quiz.

RESPONDING TO *The Harlem Renaissance*

Essential Question WHAT WAS THE HARLEM RENAISSANCE?

Reflecting on this book as a whole provides an opportunity for independent learning and the application of the critical thinking skill, synthesis. *Synthesizing* means examining all the things you have learned from this book and combining them to form a richer and more meaningful view of the Harlem Renaissance.

There are many ways to demonstrate what you know about the Harlem Renaissance. Here are some possibilities. Your teacher may provide others.

1. After reading this book you should have a better understanding of the people, literature, and attitudes that evolved during the Harlem Renaissance. Write a short essay that synthesizes what you have learned about the Harlem Renaissance and its effects on those who lived through it, as well as its effects on people today.

2. Research a Harlem Renaissance artist (consider vocalists, instrumentalists, painters, photographers, writers, poets, etc.). Create a multimedia report that features the work of your artist. If possible, several students could combine reports to create a Harlem Renaissance Arts Festival.

CLOSE READING

Re-reading, we find a new book. —Mason Cooley

Close reading is the careful interpretation of a text. Re-reading is the key strategy for close reading. The "new book" readers often encounter on re-reading is layered with meaning.

There is no single right way to do a close reading of a text. The following general process, however, presents three broad stages or levels in re-reading that build on one another to help produce a deep understanding of a text.

1. First Readings: Build Understanding

On a first reading, focus on grasping the literal or explicit meaning of a text. Answer the questions as you read, paraphrase key ideas, and jot down any questions you have.

Informational Text	
Questions to Ask	**Where to Look for Answers**
What is the main idea?	Title, introduction, or first few paragraphs
What information backs up the main idea?	Body paragraphs, especially their topic sentences
How are the ideas in the text related to one another?	Transitions between sections/ideas
What conclusion does the writer draw, and how does it relate to the main idea and supporting ideas?	Concluding paragraphs

Argumentative Text	
Questions to Ask	**Where to Look for Answers**
What is the main claim, or point the writer is trying to prove?	Title, introduction, or first few paragraphs
What evidence does the writer provide to back up that claim?	Body paragraphs, especially their topic sentences
What counterclaims, if any, does the writer address?	Body paragraphs, often marked with such words and phrases as "in contrast," "despite," "while it is true that"
How are the ideas in the text related to one another?	Transitions between sections/ideas
What conclusion does the writer draw, and how does it relate to the main claim and supporting ideas?	Concluding paragraphs

Narrative Text	
Questions to Ask	Where to Look for Answers
What event starts the narrative in motion?	Introduction or first few paragraphs
What is the setting of the narrative?	Introduction and throughout
Who are the people or characters in the narrative?	Introduction and throughout
What problem do the people or characters face?	Introduction and throughout
What happens to the people or characters as the narrative unfolds?	Body paragraphs
What is the outcome or resolution of the narrative?	Concluding paragraphs

Poetry	
Questions to Ask	Where to Look for Answers
If the poem tells a story, what is the basic outline of that story?	Throughout
What is the tone of the poem?	Throughout
What images, words, or ideas stand out as striking?	Throughout
What images, words, or ideas are repeated, if any?	Throughout
What message do you see in the poem?	Title, throughout

2. Focused Re-readings: Analyze the Text and Gather Evidence

Re-reading after you have grasped a basic understanding of a text is the stage at which you are most likely to encounter that "new book" referred to in the beginning quote, because at this level you analyze the text carefully and focus on details that may bring new meaning to what you have read. The chart below shows some of the points you can focus on in a re-reading of almost any kind of text. It also shows what questions you can ask and where and how you can discover the answers to those questions.

Focused Re-reading		
Focus and Thinking Skills	Questions to Ask	Finding Textual Evidence
Author's purpose, such as to inform, put forward an argument, entertain, satirize, tell a story *Thinking skills: Recognize explicit statements; draw inferences about implied purpose(s)*	Why did the writer write this? Is the purpose stated explicitly or is it only implied?	Look in the title and beginning paragraphs for quotes that show the answers to your questions.

continued

Focus and Thinking Skills	Questions to Ask	Finding Textual Evidence
Word choice and style, including length of sentences, variety of sentence beginnings, and variety of sentence types *Thinking skills: Analyze; break passages down by word choice and sentence style and look for patterns*	What words and phrases caught your attention for their strength and clarity? Does the author tend to use long sentences, short sentences, or a variety of sentence lengths? Do the sentences begin in a variety of ways (for example, subject first, prepositional phrase first, etc.)?	Look throughout for examples that demonstrate the results of your analysis (for example, three vivid word choices, three varied sentence patterns, etc.). In a long text, examine a section from the beginning, two or three sections from the middle, and a section from the end.
Figurative language, such as similes, metaphors, hyperbole, alliteration *Thinking skills: Analyze to identify figures of speech; classify the type of figurative language; compare figurative language to a possible replacement in literal language*	What figures of speech does the writer use? What do they accomplish that literal language would not?	Look throughout, but especially in descriptive passages, for various examples of figurative language and compare them to literal language.
Structure, including main sections and such organizational patterns as chronological order and order of importance *Thinking skills: Analyze to identify the sections of a text; classify to determine the organizational pattern*	What are the main sections of the text? What is the organizational pattern of the text?	Look throughout the text for transitional words and phrases that show both where sections break and how they are connected. Identify the main ideas from each section.
Point of view in fiction, including choice of narrator *Thinking skills: Analyze narrative to identify point of view; compare points of view by imagining a passage told from a different point of view and evaluating the effect.*	Is the story told from the first- or third-person point of view? If it is not in first-person, how much does the narrator know about the characters? What effect does the choice of narrative point of view have on the text? Why might the author have chosen that point of view?	Look for pronouns. If the narrator refers to himself or herself as "I," the story is in first-person. Look at key passages in which important information is revealed for examples that show the effect of point of view on the narrative.

continued

Focused Re-reading *(cont.)*		
Focus and Thinking Skills	**Questions to Ask**	**Finding Textual Evidence**
Point of view in nonfiction, including frame of reference, such as scientist, parent, teenager *Thinking skills: Recognize explicit statements; draw inferences about the writer from telling details*	What is the writer's frame of reference?	Look in the introduction and body paragraphs for details that give insight into the writer's experience, worldview, and possible bias.
Implied meanings *Thinking skills: Analyze details; draw inferences and conclusions*	What is left unsaid? What inference can you draw from a collection of details when you "read between the lines"?	Look throughout for details that "show" not "tell." In fiction these would include the actions of the characters and details of the setting. In nonfiction, these might appear in descriptive passages where the reader is left to draw his or her own conclusions. Find examples that support your interpretation of the implied meaning.

Different kinds of texts suggest additional points to focus on during re-reading.

Focused Re-Reading of Informational and Argumentative Text		
Focus and Thinking Skills	**Questions to Ask**	**Finding Textual Evidence**
Clarification and verification of information *Thinking skills: Define key terms; analyze complicated sentences and paragraphs; compare to other sources to verify information*	What parts confused you? What did you not understand well on first reading? What seemed to contradict information you thought you knew?	Look in passages that raised questions in your mind in first reading; refer to outside sources if necessary for confirming or contradicting information.
Assumptions *Thinking skills: Logical thinking to evaluate the assumption underlying the claim*	Does every claim depend on a valid assumption?	Look for passages that put forward claims in an argument; look for examples, if any, of hidden assumptions.

continued

Focused Re-Reading of Informational and Argumentative Text *(cont.)*		
Focus and Thinking Skills	**Questions to Ask**	**Finding Textual Evidence**
Development of an argument and key supporting ideas *Thinking skills: Evaluate the relevance, sufficiency, and importance of the supporting details; distinguish fact from opinion*	By what method does the writer attempt to prove his or her point? Are the supporting ideas relevant and sufficient to prove the point?	Look throughout for all the facts, reasons, and examples offered in support of each claim and/or counterclaim.
Style and tone *Thinking skills: Analyze language choices; evaluate appropriateness*	Is the style formal and respectful, or informal and full of "loaded" language (words that carry strong, usually negative connotations)?	Look throughout, but especially at the beginning and ending where the author wants to make his or her point most strongly, for examples that show formal, respectful language or disrespectful loaded language.

Focused Re-reading of Fiction and Drama		
Focus and Thinking Skills	**Questions to Ask**	**Finding Textual Evidence**
Plot *Thinking skills: Sequence; draw inferences; examine cause-effect relationships*	What is the impact of each main development of the plot on the characters?	Look for examples of characters' words or actions before a turning point in the story and after a turning point.
Setting *Thinking skills: Draw inferences*	How does the setting contribute to the mood of the story? How do the details of the setting help define characters?	Look for descriptive details throughout the story about the time and physical characteristics of the place of the events and their impact on mood and characters.
Characters *Thinking skills: Analyze details of characterization; generalize from details; draw inferences from details*	How does each character contribute to the development of the plot? How do the details of characterization and the dialogue reveal the characters' personalities and motivations? Why do characters act as they do?	Look throughout for character 1) descriptions, 2) thoughts, 3) words, 4) actions, 5) changes, 6) motivations.
Theme *Thinking skills: Draw inferences; generalize from details; synthesize various elements*	How does the author communicate the theme through the development of setting, characters, and plot? What passages and details in the story best express the main theme?	Look for passages and details from each main part of the story or drama that express theme.

Focused Re-reading of Poetry		
Focus and Thinking Skills	**Questions to Ask**	**Finding Textual Evidence**
Persona (the poet's "voice") *Thinking skills: Analyze; draw inferences*	How does the persona relate to the subject, mood, and theme of the poem?	Look for specific examples that show the persona's involvement and reveal attitudes.
Meter and rhyme *Thinking skills: Analyze meter and rhyme; synthesize to assess their effect*	How do the meter and rhyme affect the rhythm and mood of the poem?	Look for metrical patterns and rhyme schemes from several places in the poem.
Sound devices, such as alliteration, assonance, onomatopoeia *Thinking skills: Analyze language; classify types of sound devices; draw inferences about their meaning and effect*	What sound devices are in the poem? What effect do they have?	Look throughout the poem for examples of sound devices in relation to other elements of the poem.
Theme *Thinking skills: Draw inferences; generalize from details; synthesize various elements*	How does the poet communicate the theme through the details of the poem?	Look for passages and details from throughout the poem that express theme.

3. Synthesis: Evaluate the Text

By now you may have encountered the "new book" that close reading often reveals, a text with layers of meaning. On later re-readings, you can stand back from the text and begin to see it from a critic's point of view. Following are some of the criteria by which any great work of literature, or classic, is usually judged. When you evaluate a literary work, nonfiction or fiction, consider the following characteristics.

Some Characteristics of Great Literature
• Explores great themes in human nature and the human experience that many people can identify with—such as growing up, family life, personal struggles, or war
• Expresses universal values—such as truth or hope—to which people from many different backgrounds and cultures can relate
• Conveys a timeless message that remains true for many generations of readers
• Presents vivid impressions of characters, settings, and situations that many generations of readers can treasure
• Demonstrates outstanding and inventive understanding of important aspects of humanity and society

The chart below shows some questions you can ask—and answer with evidence from the text—when you are evaluating a text.

Questions for Evaluating a Text	
Informational Text	How effectively has the writer • presented a clear explanation on a topic of value • used examples and other supporting details • accurately conveyed information • structured the explanation • used language and style to add clarity and life • presented an unbiased view • engaged the reader
Argumentative Writing	How effectively has the writer • presented a clear position or claim on a subject of importance • used examples and other details to support claims • accurately conveyed information • addressed counterclaims • used logic • covered the topic in sufficient depth and breadth • been fair-minded • structured the argument • used language and style to add clarity and life • convinced you
Fiction and Drama	How effectively has the writer • drawn well-rounded characters worth getting to know • developed and paced a plot • set mood and tone • used language • structured the story • developed a meaningful theme
Poetry	How effectively has the poet • used (or not used) rhyme • created stunning word pictures • used figurative language • structured the poem • expressed an otherwise inexpressible idea

USING TEXTUAL EVIDENCE

Prove it! Anytime you write a literary analysis, informational text, or argument, you will be expected to prove your main idea or claim. You draw the **textual evidence** for that proof from the collection of details you have mined during your close readings.

During your close readings, you gathered evidence by taking notes from the work itself. These notes may have included descriptive passages, lines of dialogue, narrative details, facts, examples, statistics, and other kinds of details. In drafting an analysis of a text or in piecing together an informational or argumentative text from several sources, include the evidence in a way that will convince readers of your main idea or claim.

Strengthen your arguments by using relevant quotations from your text or texts that support a point. Work them smoothly into your writing and punctuate them correctly. The following guidelines show how to work textual evidence into a written analysis. They use examples from a literary analysis on a short story by Marjorie Kinnan Rawlings called "A Mother in Mannville."

Guidelines for Using Direct Quotations in a Literary Analysis

1. Always enclose direct quotations in quotation marks.
2. Follow the examples below when writing quotations in different positions in the sentence. Notice that quotations in the middle or end of a sentence are not ordinarily capitalized.

Begins Sentence	"He wore overalls and a torn shirt," observes the narrator (323).
Interrupts Sentence	In his "grave gray-blue eyes," the narrator sees a rare and precious quality (325).
Ends Sentence	The narrator feels that Jerry's integrity makes him "more than brave" (325).

3. Use ellipses—a series of three dots (. . .)—to show that words have been left out of a quotation.

    "For a moment, finding that he had a mother shocked me . . . and I did not know why it disturbed me" (327).
4. If the quotation is four lines or longer, set it off by itself without quotation marks. Indent one inch on the left and leave space above and below it.

    > And after my first fury at her—we did not speak of
    > her again—his having a mother, any sort at all, not far
    > away, in Mannville, relieved me of the ache I had had
    > about him. . . . He was not lonely. It was none of my
    > concern. (328)

5. After each quotation cite the page number of the text in parentheses. The citation usually precedes punctuation marks such as periods, commas, colons, and semicolons. For plays or long poems, also give main divisions, such as the act and scene of the play or the part of the poem, plus line numbers.

Following are examples of using textual evidence in a different kind of writing—an informational research report on the lost city of Atlantis. The sources are indicated in parentheses and would be keyed to a works-cited page at the end of the report.

Examples of Using Textual Evidence in an Informational Report

1. Use a quotation to finish a sentence you have started.

   Example Photographs taken in 1977 of underwater stones are believed to "bear the mark of human handiwork" (Whitney).

2. Quote a whole sentence. If you omit words from a sentence, indicate the omission with an ellipsis, a series of three dots (. . .).

   Example "He suggests that the structures match the description in Plato's Dialogue Critias . . . and that the high mountains of Atlantis are actually those of the Sierra Morena and the Sierra Nevada" (Shermer).

3. Quote four or more lines from a source. For a quotation of this length, skip two lines and set the quotation as a block indented one inch on the left. You do not need quotation marks for such an extended quotation.

   Example Here is how Plato describes the downfall of Atlantis in the dialogue called *Timaeus:*

   Some time later excessively violent earthquakes and floods occurred, and after the onset of an unbearable day and a night, your entire warrior force sank below the earth all at once, and the Isle of Atlantis likewise sank below the sea and disappeared. (1232)

4. Quote just a few words.

   Example According to Plato, in an "unbearable day and a night" Atlantis was destroyed (*Timaeus* 1232).

5. Paraphrase information from a source.

   Example "Although many have dismissed Atlantis as a myth, some 50,000 volumes have been written to describe and locate it." [Original]
   Curiosity about Atlantis and efforts to locate it gave rise to some 50,000 books on the topic ("Greek Backs Plato Theory"). [paraphrase]

For informational and argumentative texts, including research reports, be sure to verify factual evidence in your sources for accuracy.

Verifying Factual Evidence
• Locate at least two sources that contain the same basic facts.
• Skim each source for specific details, such as dates, locations, and statistics.
• If the specific details in both sources agree, you can probably rely on their accuracy.
• Watch for discrepancies in broader concepts, such as in the sequence of events or in the relationship between cause and effect.
• If you discover discrepancies, use a third source to determine which source is likely to be more accurate.

COMPARING TEXTS

Another way to achieve a deep understanding of a text is to compare it to another text. You can compare and contrast literary texts in many ways. You could, for example, do a close reading of two (or more) texts using any of the same focus points outlined on pages 144–148, and then compare and contrast the way each text addresses that focus point. Following are just a few of many examples.

Two or More Texts of This Type	Focus Points to Compare and Contrast
Short stories	Structure (use of chronological order or flashbacks), theme, plot, character development, point of view, setting, style
Poems	Role of persona, figurative language, rhyme and meter, theme
Biographies	Details of life that are emphasized or omitted in each version; overall sense of person's character and motivation
Informational Texts	Structure, point of view, importance of main idea, support for main idea, language and style, author's purpose, accuracy of information, possible bias
Argumentative Texts	Structure, point of view, significance of main claim, quality of supporting details for claims, logical reasoning, accuracy of information, possible bias, language and style, conclusions

The following chart shows additional ways to compare and contrast texts to deepen your understanding of them.

Types of Texts to Compare	Questions for Comparing Texts
Texts in different forms or genres (such as stories and poems, historical novels and fantasy stories, short stories and novels)	• How is the approach to theme and topic similar in both forms? • How is the approach to theme and topic different in the two forms or genres? • How does their form or genre make these texts unique?
Fictional portrayal of a time, place, or character and a historical account of the same period	• How do authors of fiction use or alter history?
Modern work of fiction versus traditional sources	• In what ways does the modern work draw on themes, patterns of events, or character types from myths, traditional stories, or religious works? • How is the modern work turned into something new and fresh?

continued

Types of Texts to Compare (cont.)	Questions for Comparing Texts (cont.)
Texts from the same era that approach themes differently	• What was the purpose of each text? • What was the writer's frame of reference or worldview? • Whom was the writer addressing ?
Texts from different eras	• What does each text reveal about social attitudes during the time in which it was written?
Different texts by the same author	• What themes appear repeatedly in works by this author? • What changes in style and/or theme, if any, are apparent in later works by the author compared to earlier works?

Comparing Texts in Different Mediums "Texts" do not necessarily need to be written pieces. In fact, comparing texts in different mediums—such as print, audio, and video—can lead to valuable insights.

The following chart shows some questions to ask when comparing and contrasting texts in different mediums.

Reading a Story, Drama, or Poem	Listening to or Viewing an Audio, Video, or Live Version of the Text
• When you read the text, what do you see in your mind's eye? How do you picture the visual images, the characters, and the setting? • What do you hear—what do the characters' voices sound like? • What are the sounds in the setting? • What can you experience reading a text that you cannot experience when viewing or listening to an audio, video, or live version of the text?	• When you listen to an audio version of the text, what do you experience in comparison to when you read it? Are any elements more vivid? less vivid? • When you view a video version of the text, what do you experience in comparison to when you read it? • What can a video provide that a written text cannot? • How does the experience of a live performance differ from reading a text? • What can a live performance offer that reading a text cannot? • How faithful to the original text is the audio, video, or live version? If it differs in significant ways, why do you think the directors and actors made the choices they did to change it?

You know the techniques writers use to make an impression and impact. They include provocative language, narration that can get inside of characters' heads, and plenty of room for the readers' imaginations to fill in visual and auditory details. Understanding the "tools of the trade" of different mediums can help you make clear comparisons and contrasts.

Techniques of Audio	Techniques of Video	Techniques of Stage
• Actual voices and other sounds in the setting • Possibility of music to help create mood • Room for imagination to fill in visual aspects	• Representation of all sounds and visuals; little left to the imagination • Lighting, sound recording, camera angles, color, focus, and special effects all shape the visual message • Use of background music to help create mood • Editing techniques that place one scene next to another to make a comment	• Representation of some sounds and visuals within the limited scope of the stage • Stage directions that tell characters how to interact in each scene • Lighting and other special effects • Live actors creating a sense of immediacy • Use of music

Sometimes you may be asked to **compare a single scene in two different mediums.** For example, a chilling scene in the book *To Kill a Mockingbird* centers on the shooting of a mad dog by mild-mannered lawyer Atticus Finch. If you read that scene carefully in the book and then compared and contrasted it to the same scene in the movie version of the book, you could evaluate what is emphasized or absent in each treatment of the scene.

Sometimes you may be asked to **compare multiple versions of a story, drama, or poem in different mediums.** How does the stage version of *To Kill a Mockingbird* differ from both the print and movie versions? How do the film and stage versions offer different interpretations of the original text?

AUTHOR BIOGRAPHIES

JERVIS ANDERSON Born in Jamaica in 1932, Jervis Anderson spent most of his adult life in New York City. A writer of biographies and of social and cultural history, Anderson first won recognition for his biographies of African-American civil rights leaders Bayard Rustin and A. Philip Randolph. He also wrote shorter biographies, including a profile of Ralph Ellison, which was published in the *New Yorker.* Anderson worked as a staff writer for the *New Yorker* from 1968 until 1998. Critic Darryl Pinckney has called Anderson's book *This Was Harlem* a "valuable primer" on the Harlem Renaissance. Anderson died in New York City in 2000.

JAMES BALDWIN The oldest of nine children, James Baldwin was born in Harlem in 1924. His mother was a domestic worker; he never knew his biological father. He took the surname of his stepfather, a stern man who was both a preacher and a factory worker. Baldwin himself served as a storefront preacher for three years, beginning at age fourteen. He began his first novel shortly after finishing high school, and in 1943 he began writing full-time. His work was rejected repeatedly, but he earned a living writing essays and book reviews. Baldwin finally found critical acclaim in 1953, with the publication of the somewhat autobiographical *Go Tell It on the Mountain.* Since then, his novels, poetry, and essays have won praise and a number of prizes, including a Guggenheim Fellowship. Baldwin continued to write throughout his adult life and also became active in the Civil Rights Movement. In 1983, he accepted a position as a professor at the University of Massachusetts. Later, he moved to France, where he died in 1987.

ARNA BONTEMPS was born in Louisiana in 1902. When he was three years old, he moved with his family to Los Angeles, California. His parents emphasized education, and Bontemps finished college in three years. The year after he graduated, he published his first poem. Over time, Bontemps published 25 books on various topics ranging from poetry to history. He also taught at a private school in Harlem and, with his wife, raised six children. In 1969, Bontemps became head librarian at Fisk University and curator of the James Weldon Johnson Memorial Collection at Yale. He died in 1973.

FRANK BYRD In his work for the Federal Writers Project during the Great Depression, writer Frank Byrd chronicled the life of poor blacks in New York City. Byrd wrote about the migration of 200,000 African Americans from the South to New York City in search of factory jobs. He interviewed countless individuals and described in vivid detail the rent parties that allowed the residents of Harlem to pay the rent and also invigorated the social and literary scene there. He highlighted significant personalities in Harlem and memorialized a community that grew out of a slum.

COUNTEE CULLEN A significant poet of his time, Countee Cullen was also a cornerstone figure of the Harlem Renaissance. His early life is shrouded in mystery; biographers are sure only that he was born in 1903 and adopted in 1918 by Frederick and Carolyn Cullen. While still in high school, Cullen won a prize for his poetry. In 1925, while a senior in college, he published his first book of poems and found critical acclaim. Throughout the 1920s, Cullen won numerous prizes for his work, including a Guggenheim Fellowship. During the 1930s, Cullen taught French and English at Frederick Douglass Jr. High School in New York. There, he met and mentored James Baldwin. Cullen died in 1946. In later years his fame was eclipsed by that of Langston Hughes and others, but a renewed interest in his poetry has led publishers to reissue some of his best work.

CAROLINE BOND DAY Born in 1889, Caroline Bond Day is thought to be the first African American to earn a Ph.D. in anthropology. By producing genealogical information about interracial families in the American South, she revealed the "color line" between blacks and whites to be a false construct. Day's work helped break down opposition to interracial marriage. It also garnered respect for African American women, whose role as caretaker helped stabilize and support African American families. In addition to establishing herself as a prominent physical anthropologist, Day earned a place in Boston's local history as a leader of the black YWCA. She died in 1948.

W. E. B. DU BOIS Born in Massachusetts in 1868, W. E. B. Du Bois was the first African American to earn a Ph. D. from Harvard. Du Bois went on to teach, eventually founding the sociology department at Atlanta University. He wrote and lectured tirelessly, authoring countless books and articles about the African-American experience. A founding member of both the Niagara Movement to end segregation and the NAACP, Du Bois also edited the NAACP's magazine *The Crisis,* which launched careers for many writers of the Harlem Renaissance. Du Bois was publicly denounced as a traitor during the McCarthy era, but he was later vindicated as an important contributor to African-American culture in particular and American culture in general. In 1963, the man who has been called "one of the greatest scholars in American history" died a citizen of Ghana, his adopted home.

MAURICE E. DUHON, JR. wrote as a teenager about the influence the Harlem Renaissance had upon him. His prose poem *There's a Harlem Renaissance in My Head* is an homage to Langston Hughes, Duke Ellington, and others who developed a tradition from which his own artistic vision could grow.

RUDOLPH FISHER Born in 1897 in Washington D.C., Rudolph Fisher grew up in Rhode Island. He would have been a "Renaissance man" even if there had been no Harlem Renaissance. The son of a physician, Fisher himself became a physician and an X-ray specialist. He also was a playwright, novelist, short story writer, musician, and orator. Fisher won prizes for oratory throughout his undergraduate career at Brown University, where he studied both English and biology. He earned a medical degree from Howard University in 1924. Fisher is best known for his novels and short stories, but he also was a talented musician. In fact, he arranged several of the songs Paul Robeson performed in his first New York concert. Fisher died of cancer in 1934 at the age of 37. Despite his short life, he made a lasting contribution to the Harlem Renaissance.

E. FRANKLIN FRAZIER The son of a bank messenger, E. Franklin Frazier was born in Baltimore in 1894. He graduated from Howard University, and in 1916 began teaching high school history, mathematics, and modern languages. Inspired by the work of W. E. B. Du Bois, he embarked upon graduate studies and a career as a sociologist in 1919. In 1932, he earned a Ph.D. from the University of Chicago. Frazier's studies of African-American life earned him widespread admiration, and in 1948, he became the first African-American president of the American Sociological Association. As he continued his studies of African Americans, he became convinced of the importance of children's having a stable, two-parent home and of adults participating in social activism. Later in life, Frazier expressed his indebtedness toDu Bois by showing public support for him throughout the McCarthy era. He died in 1962.

MARCUS GARVEY Born in Jamaica in 1887, Marcus Garvey helped launch the racial pride movement that inspired the Harlem Renaissance. Garvey began his working life at age fourteen, when he took a job as a printer's apprentice. An active participant in Jamaica's nationalist movement, he traveled widely and developed an international awareness and a commitment to social activism. He brought both these assets with him when he arrived in the United States in 1916. Garvey founded American chapters of both the Universal Negro Improvement Association (UNIA) and the African Communities League (ACL), which worked for both racial pride and economic independence. He also founded a black-owned shipping line and a newspaper.

EDDY L. HARRIS A graduate of Stanford University, Eddy L. Harris studied in London and lives in St. Louis, Missouri. He is considered a preeminent African- American travel and memoir author. His critically praised books, among them *Mississippi Solo*, *Native Stranger*, and *Still Life in Harlem*, strike chords of deep emotion and courage. His book *Mississippi Solo* details Harris's solo voyage (in a borrowed canoe) on the Mississippi from Minnesota through Missouri and on to New Orleans.

LANGSTON HUGHES Born in 1902 in Joplin, Missouri, and raised mostly in Lawrence, Kansas, Langston Hughes grew up in a family that had been actively involved in the abolitionist movement. Left alone more than he liked, he turned to reading and writing. By the time Hughes enrolled at Columbia University, he had already published a significant poem and was committed to a career as a writer. After college, Hughes traveled aboard a steamer for several years. When he returned to the United States, he embarked on his first novel, with the support of patron Charlotte Mason. That relationship ended badly, but Hughes continued to write. Though he is known mostly for his unforgettable poetry, he also established a reputation as a fiction writer, journalist, lyricist, and children's writer. In addition, he wrote a weekly column for the *Chicago Defender*. Hughes was always frank about his views, and he became a target of McCarthy-era radical conservatives. Yet he continued to write until his death in 1967. Hughes has been called "the poet laureate of Harlem," but his fame and influence extend across the globe.

ZORA NEALE HURSTON Born in 1891 in Eatonville, Florida, Zora Neale Hurston was educated at Howard University, Barnard, and Columbia University. She began her career as a folklorist, collecting and retelling African and African-American tales in Jamaica, Haiti, Bermuda, Florida, and Honduras. She also wrote stories, novels, and an autobiography. Hurston experienced a markedly split reaction to her work. Though some writers and readers appreciated her work, others were uncomfortable with the bawdiness of her stories. Still others resented Hurston's lack of interest in social activism. Many were offended by her opposition to integration and her suggestion that African Americans should seek social and cultural sovereignty. Thus, Hurston's fortunes fell. After enjoying several years of fame, she sank into obscurity. When she died in 1960, she was penniless and largely forgotten, but scholars and writers have taken up a renewed interest in her work.

SPIKE LEE Born Sheldon Jackson Lee in 1957 in Atlanta, Georgia, Spike Lee's father was a jazz composer and his mother was an art teacher. The oldest of four children, He was nicknamed Spike by his mother. The Lee family moved from Atlanta to Chicago and then to New York, where the parents immersed their children in the cultural richness of the city. Though Lee's undergraduate efforts did not meet with much encouragement, he earned a master's degree in filmmaking at NYU in 1982. In 1983, he won the Student Academy Award for Best Director. The award did not result in work, however, and so Lee took a job at a distribution house and began trying to raise money to finance his filmmaking. After a painful false start, Lee began producing and distributing intense, controversial films about race and culture in the United States. He became known as a multitalented filmmaker who writes, directs, produces, and appears in his work. Today, Lee is internationally known. He also directs and appears in commercials and music videos and is the founder of a minority scholarship at NYU's Tisch School of the Arts.

JANET MABIE was a journalist who worked for the *Christian Science Monitor.* Her work praising Duke Ellington's personal virtues helped cement his nationwide reputation. Mabie also wrote a biography of her friend Amelia Earhart, which remained unpublished but was recently rediscovered. Her work became in important source of information about the pioneering aviator. Through her work as a journalist, Mabie attained a level of authority rare for African-American women in the early twentieth century.

CLAUDE MCKAY Born in Jamaica in 1890, Claude McKay was the youngest of eleven children. Early in life he was sent to live with his oldest brother, a schoolteacher. McKay began writing poetry at age ten, but planned to enter a trade in order to make a living. After several years in various apprenticeships, McKay found a mentor in Englishman Walter Jekyll, who encouraged him to write poetry in dialect. McKay moved to the United States in 1912. At first, he could not make a living as a writer, so he worked at menial jobs in order to support himself, but eventually, his lyric poems earned him recognition and respect. McKay worked as a journalist for left-wing publications in the early 1920s, then began publishing novels and an autobiography, as well as poems. He traveled whenever his finances allowed. An influential figure of the Harlem Renaissance, Claude McKay died in 1948.

VIVIAN MORRIS Unlike Frank Byrd, Ralph Ellison, and others, Vivian Morris was an unknown when she won a WPA assignment to document life in Harlem. Nevertheless, her compelling portraits of African-American life and folklore during the Depression helped to illuminate life in Harlem during the 1930s.

ALICE WALKER The youngest of eight children, Alice Walker was born in 1944 in Georgia to a family of sharecroppers. She lost eyesight in one eye at the age of eight when one of her brothers accidentally shot her in the eye with a BB gun. Nevertheless, Walker was an achiever all her life. In high school she was valedictorian of her class. She won a full scholarship to Spellman College and to Sarah Lawrence. Walker graduated in 1965, got married in 1967, and published her first book of poems in 1968. She also became an active participant in the Civil Rights Movement. Shortly after she gave birth to her daughter in 1970, Walker published her first novel. In 1983, she won the Pulitzer Prize for *The Color Purple,* and in 1984, launched her own publishing company, Wild Trees Press. Currently, she lives in Northern California, where she continues to write and work for human and civil rights.

DOROTHY WEST As a teenager, Dorothy West was an active presence during the Harlem Renaissance. She became the last surviving member of that august group. Not long after graduating from Girls' Latin School in Boston in 1926, she tied for a second-place prize in a short story contest. The other second-place winner was Zora Neale Hurston. Hurston became her friend and encouraged her to leave Boston for New York. In New York, West was befriended by such luminaries as Langston Hughes and Richard Wright. In 1948 she published her first book, *The Living Is Easy.* "We didn't know it was the Harlem Renaissance . . . we were all young and all poor," West said in 1995. "We had no jobs to speak of, and we had rent parties to raise rent money." At the age of 88, West's second novel, *The Wedding,* was published. It was very successful, and soon *The Richer, The Poorer,* her collection of short stories, was in bookstores. Dorothy West died in 1998 at the age of 97.

Acknowledgments

TEXT CREDITS CONTINUED FROM PAGE 2 from "Ellington's 'Mood in Indigo': Harlem's 'Duke' Seeks to Express His Race," by Janet Mabie. This article first appeared in *The Christian Science Monitor* on December 13, 1930, and is reproduced with permission. Copyright © 1930 *The Christian Science Monitor.* All rights reserved.

"Harlem Wine" by Countee Cullen. Copyrights administered by Thompson and Thompson, New York, NY.

"How It Feels to Be Colored Me" by Zora Neale Hurston. Used with permission of the estate of Zora Neale Hurston.

"If Black English Isn't a Language, Then Tell Me, What Is?" by James Baldwin from *The New York Times.* Copyright © July 29, 1979, by the New York Times Co. Reprinted by permission.

"In Search of Zora Neale Hurston" from *In Search of Our Mothers' Gardens: Womanist Prose,* copyright © 1975 by Alice Walker, reprinted by permission of Harcourt, Inc.

"Jazzonia" from *The Collected Poems of Langston Hughes* by Langston Hughes, copyright © 1994 by the Estate of Langston Hughes. Used by permission of Alfred A. Knopf, a division of Random House, Inc.

"The Negro Artist and the Racial Mountain" by Langston Hughes. Reprinted by permission of Harold Ober Associates Incorporated. Copyright © 1926 by Langston Hughes. Copyright renewed.

"The Negro Speaks of Rivers" from *Collected Poems* by Langston Hughes. Copyright © 1994 by the Estate of Langston Hughes. Reprinted by permission of Alfred A. Knopf, a Division of Random House Inc.

"The Pink Hat" by Caroline Bond Day from *Harlem's Glory: Black Women Writing,* © 1996. Reprinted by permission of the National Urban League.

"Race Pride" by W. E. B. Du Bois from *The Crisis,* Vol. XIX, © 1920. The publisher wishes to thank The Crisis Publishing Co., Inc., the publisher of the magazine of the National Association for the Advancement of Colored People, for the use of this work.

"Seventh Avenue: The Great Black Way" from *This Was Harlem: A Cultural Portrait,* 1900-1950 by Jervis Anderson. Copyright © 1982 by Jervis Anderson. Reprinted by permission of Farrar, Straus and Giroux, LLC.

"Spike's Gotta Do It" by Spike Lee. Excerpted with permission of Simon & Schuster from *Spike Lee's Gotta Have It: Inside Guerrilla Filmmaking* by Spike Lee. Copyright © 1987 by Spike Lee.

from *Still Life in Harlem* by Eddy L. Harris. Copyright © 1996 by Eddy L. Harris. Reprinted by permission of Henry Holt and Company, LLC.

"The Tropics in New York," by Claude McKay from *The Poetry of the Negro: 1746-1970,* copyright © 1970. Used by permission of Random House, Inc.

Every reasonable effort has been made to properly acknowledge ownership of all material used. Any omissions or mistakes are unintentional and, if brought to the publisher's attention, will be corrected in future editions.

PHOTO AND ART CREDITS Cover (Detail) and Title Page: Winold Reiss, *Interpretation of Harlem Jazz I*, ca. 1925. Ink on paper, 20 x 15 inches. Private collection. Reproduced with permission. Page 5: Aaron Douglas, *To Midnight Nan at Leroy's*, from *Opportunity* magazine, January, 1926. © National Urban League. Page 9: T, James Van Der Zee, *Renaissance Casino*, 1927. Copyright © Donna Mussenden Van Der Zee; B, The Granger Collection. Page 10: T, James Van Der Zee, *Self-portrait*, c. 1921. Copyright © Donna Mussenden Van Der Zee; B, National Museum of American Art, Smithsonian Institution, Washington, D.C., The Schomburg Center for Research in Black Culture, The New York Public Library, NY/Art Resource, NY. Page 11: L, The Granger Collection; R, Aaron Douglas, *Self-portrait*, from *Opportunity* magazine, September, 1925. © National Urban League. Page 12: T, Richard Hadlock Collection; M, Brown Brothers; B, James Latimer Allen, *Portrait of Jacob Lawrence*. Gelatin silver print ca. 1937-1939. Alain Locke Collection, Moorland-Spingarn Research Center, Howard University. Page 13: T, The Granger Collection; M and Page 67: Carl Van Vechten. Reproduced with permission from the Van Vechten Trust. Photo from Yale collection of American Literature, Beinecke Rare Book & Manuscript Library; BL, Hulton Getty/Archive Photos; BR and Page 100, Frank Driggs/Archive Photos. Page 14: T and M, Carl Van Vechten, The Studio Museum in Harlem. Page 15: © Bettmann/Corbis. Page 17: James Van Der Zee, *Parade Along Seventh Avenue*, c. 1924. Copyright © Donna Mussenden Van Der Zee. Page 18: L, Perfection Learning Corporation wishes to thank The Crisis Publishing Co., Inc., the publisher of the magazine of the National Association for the Advancement of Colored People, for the use of this work; R, Culver Pictures, Inc. Page 19: Robert Riggs, *The Brown Bomber*, 1938. 31 x 41 inches. The Art Museum of Western Virginia, Roanoke, VA. Acquired with funds provided by the Horace G. Fralin Charitable Trust, 2000.03. Page 20: James Van Der Zee, *Portrait of Couple, Man with Walking Stick*, 1924. Copyright © Donna Mussenden Van Der Zee. Page 21: James Van Der Zee, *Couple in Raccoon Coats*, 1932. Copyright © Donna Mussenden Van Der Zee. Page 22: Leigh Richmond Miner, *Portia Ironing*, 1907. Collection of Hampton University Archives. Page 26: William H. Johnson, *Man in a Vest*, ca. 1939. Smithsonian American Art Museum, Washington, D.C./Art Resource, NY. Page 35: Winold Reiss, *Elise Johnson McDougald*, ca. 1924. National Portrait Gallery, Smithsonian Institution/Art Resource, NY. Page 36: Archibald J. Motley, Jr., *Street Scene, Chicago*, 1936. Oil on canvas, 36 x 42 inches. © Archie Motley, courtesy of Michael Rosenfeld Gallery, NY. Page 44: Aaron Douglas, *Aspects of Negro Life: The Negro in an African Setting*, 1934. (Detail) Oil on canvas. Arts and Artifacts Collection, Schomburg Center for Research in Black Culture, The New York Public Library, NY/Art Resource, NY. Page 45: Archibald J. Motley, Jr., *Blues*, 1929. (Detail and Complete) Oil on canvas, 80 x 100.3 inches. Collection of Archie Motley and Valerie Gerrard Browne. © Archie Motley, photo courtesy of Chicago Historical Society. Page 47: Winold Reiss, *Portrait of W.E.B. DuBois*. Pastel. National Portrait Gallery, Smithsonian Institution/Art Resource, NY. Page 48: Irving Penn, *Optician's Window*, New York, 1939. © 1950 (Renewed 1976) The Condé Nast Publications, Inc. Page 51: © Lewis Mail/Photonica. Page 52: Library of Congress, LC-USZ62-16767. Page 56: Selma Burke, *Jim*, n.d. Plaster, 13 inch height. The Schomburg Center for Research in Black Culture, The New York Public Library, NY/Art Resource, NY. Page 61: James Van Der Zee, *Marcus Garvey in Regalia*, 1924. Copyright © Donna Mussenden Van Der Zee. Page 62: Winold Reiss, *Two Public School Teachers* from *Four Portraits of Negro Women*, 1925. Fisk University Gallery of Art. Page 68: Humbert Howard, *Portrait of My Wife*, 1950. Oil on canvas, 32 x 24.25 inches. Collection of Howard University Gallery of Art. Page 75: Aaron Douglas, *Untitled*, (Farm Life) from *Opportunity* magazine. February, 1926. © National Urban League. Page 77: Lois Mailou Jones, *The Ascent of Ethiopia*, 1932. Oil on canvas, 23.5 x 17.25 inches. Milwaukee Art Museum, Purchase, African American Arts Acquisition Fund, matching funds from Suzanne and Richard Pieper with additional support from Arthur and Dorothy Nelle Sanders. Page 78: Winold Reiss, *Portrait of Langston Hughes*. Pastel on artist board, 76.3 x 54.9 cm. National Portrait Gallery, Smithsonian Institution, Washington, D.C./Art Resource, NY. Page 85: Jacob Lawrence, *Rooftops (No.1, This is Harlem)*, 1943. Gouache with pencil underdrawing on paper, 15 3/8 x 22 11/16 inches. Hirschhorn Museum and Sculpture Garden, Smithsonian Institution, Gift of Joseph H. Hirshhorn, 1966. Photo by Lee Stalsworth. Page 86: Ernst Ludwig Kirchner, *Tapdancing Negro*, 1914. Lithograph. Copyright (for works by E. L. Kirchner) by Ingeborg and Dr. Wolfgang Henze-Ketterer, Wichtrach, Bern. Page 103: © Bettmann/Corbis. Page 105: William H. Johnson, *Jitterbugs III*, ca. 1941. Tempera, pen and ink on paper, 14 x 19 inches. James E. Lewis Gallery, Morgan State University. Page 107: Winold Reiss, *Dawn in Harlem*, ca. 1925. Ink on paper, 20 x 15 inches. Private collection. Reproduced with permission. Page 108: The Kobal Collection. Page 114: Culver Pictures, Inc. Page 118: National Portrait Gallery, Washington D.C./Art Resource, NY. Page 120: Sara Krulwich/New York Times Co./Archive Photos. Page 123: Library of Congress, LC-USZ61-1777. Page 129: Schomburg Center for Research in Black Culture, The New York Public Library, Astor, Lenox and Tilden Foundations. Page 137: Photo by Ernie Tyner. Courtesy of the Department of Rare Books and Manuscripts, University of Florida Library. Page 139: Photo courtesy Georgia Curry/Robert E. Hemenway. Page 140: © Accra Shepp, *Ian I*, 1993. Silver gelatin emulsion on leaf.